The BUSINESS *of* PROFESSIONAL SPEAKING

Expert Advice from Top Speakers to Build Your Speaking Career

The BUSINESS of PROFESSIONAL SPEAKING

Expert Advice from Top Speakers to Build Your Speaking Career

**KATE ATKIN • ROB BROWN • MINDY GIBBINS-KLEIN
JANE GUNN • STUART HARRIS • SIMON HAZELDINE
DAVID HYNER • LEE JACKSON • EILIDH MILNES
MIKE PAGAN • FELIX A. SCHWEIKERT • JO SIMPSON
AND SIMON ZUTSHI**

Edited by
MINDY GIBBINS-KLEIN AND FELIX A. SCHWEIKERT

First published in 2013 by
Panoma Press Ltd
48 St Vincent Drive, St Albans, Herts, AL1 5SJ UK
info@panomapress.com
www.panomapress.com

Cover design by Michael Inns
Book layout by by Karen Gladwell

Printed on acid-free paper from managed forests.

ISBN 978-1-909623-30-9

Contents

Introduction

Speaking is a wonderful profession. You get to share ideas and information with an audience, and get immediate feedback and interaction. You get to educate, entertain and even inspire people. You can earn money doing what you love and talking about what matters most to you. It is no wonder that more people than ever are getting into the speaking industry.

The authors of this book wish to improve and maintain a high level of professionalism and skill in the industry, as well as helping more people to do well. An ambitious goal? Perhaps, but even if the book only manages to raise the hopes, the skills and the results of the reader just a little, it will have done its job.

The idea for this book originated on a Facebook group affiliated with the Professional Speaking Association in the UK and Ireland (PSA UKI). The discussion that sparked the idea was about the wisdom and experience held by seasoned speakers. Someone uttered that fateful phrase 'We should write a book and capture all the great ideas here.' And so the book was born.

Every contributing author is an active Member or Fellow of the PSA UKI. The main goals of the PSA are to help people who speak for a living, or for whom speaking is an important part of their job or business, to speak more and speak better. Networking with other speakers is a key part of the Association, and many collaborations have been formed by members.

We have a strong desire to keep the standard of our profession very high, so we encourage newer speakers to learn from those who have been at the coal face for a while. We hope you do learn a lot, dear reader, and that it makes you think about how you could make your speaking career even more fun and rewarding.

We all wish you the greatest success in all your endeavours and we hope to meet you soon, at a speaking convention, other event or a gig – one of ours or one of yours!

All the best,

Mindy Gibbins-Klein and Felix A. Schweikert, *Editors*
and all the authors of this book

CHAPTER ONE

Building Your Reputation as a Professional Speaker

ROB BROWN *FPSA*

> *Reputation ~ the beliefs or opinions that are generally held about someone or something.*
>
> **THE COMPACT OXFORD ENGLISH DICTIONARY**

You might be the world's greatest speaker, but if you're anonymous, then you're just a well-kept secret. When people know about you and the great presentations you deliver, you will make more money and create greater speaking opportunities. People will rave about you, pay premium to get you and treat you like royalty. They'll recommend you and rebook you. Business will come to you much more easily, with more perks and shortcuts. Your good name goes before you in ensuring that all of the best deals, speaking opportunities, promotions and projects come to you instead of your competition. In other words, you become the obvious, number one 'go to' speaker for what you do.

What Exactly Is A Reputation?

> *Reputation ~ how much respect or admiration someone or something receives, based on past behaviour or character.*
>
> **CAMBRIDGE ADVANCED LEARNER'S DICTIONARY**

Your personal reputation is simply all the things people think, feel, do or say when the come into contact with you or your name. Like beauty, it's in the eye of the beholder. You are held in high esteem (or otherwise) by others.

An authentic, stand out reputation begins on the inside - your inner 'character'. This is integral to what comes out in your branding and reputation. By aligning your inner character and values to your outer personal brand, you can begin designing and controlling the reputation you desire. This simple diagram shows the relationship between your inner character, your personal brand and your personal reputation.

Your personal brand is your public face. It's how everything on the inside comes out. Your personal brand is everything that connects you to the outside world and that comes from deep within you.

The Difference Between Character, Brand and Reputation

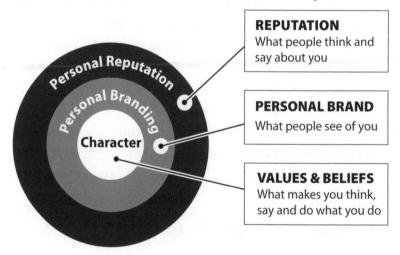

It's the outward manifestation of everything about you that comes into contact with the world. Your website, your clothes, your business card, your marketing literature, your elevator pitches, your car, your walk and your talk. These messages and cues make people think the way they do about you. You can control to some extent what others think about you, providing you give them the right messages and cues.

If you want a more snappy sound-bite for this whole reputation thing then see your reputation as your REP - the **Reason Everyone Pays**. What exactly do you want people to pay you as a professional speaker? Three things:

1. **Respect**. *That means people work with you as a partner or peer rather than supplier, provider or commodity. When people pay you a fair price for what you do, don't haggle and refer you to others.*

2. **Attention**. *In today's crowded, competitive marketplace, the challenge for you is to stand out just enough to get chosen. A formidable reputation will do that for you. It cuts through the clutter, the rhetoric and the noise so that people notice you more than everyone else.*

3. **Money**. *You might do what you do JUST for the love of it, but I doubt it. The people, performers and personalities with the best reputations will charge premium for what they do, and get it. They have a long list of interested prospects and partners. Put simply, they create the most wealth and make the most money.*

The Reason Everyone Pays

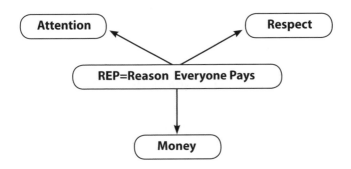

If people don't know you, they won't remember you. If they don't remember you, they won't choose you when they need what you do. I sum this up in my **FEWER** model. Having been a professional speaker for many years, it dawned on me that the speaking industry is like many others. The people at the top get the most money and the best speaking opportunities. Fewer than 10% of the professional speakers make 90% of the money. Indeed, only about 5% of the professional speakers I know personally make a six figure (£100K+) income.

Are You Easy to . . .

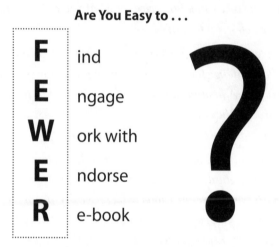

F	ind
E	ngage
W	ork with
E	ndorse
R	e-book

To be unique, you do not necessarily have to be the best, the fastest, the most knowledgeable or even the most high-profile. But you do need to distinguish yourself from the crowd in some way. You have to find a way to be 'front of mind'. You have to become the number one choice and the 'go to' professional, and that means differentiating yourself in some special way.

> *Be more aware of your character than your reputation. Your character is who you are; your reputation is merely what other people think you are.*

ANON

5 Reputation Building Tips for Professional Speakers

These 5 reputation building strategies are just some of the many in my bestselling book: **How To Build Your Reputation - The Secrets of Becoming the 'Go To' Professional in a Crowded Marketplace.**

1. **Be Brilliant!** *Being brilliant is the start of it all. This is a fantastic way to build a reputation! Get really good at something you really love doing, and people will pay you. A lot. Never underestimate the allure and the attraction of someone who is a master of their craft and the top dog in their field. Cultivate your speaking swagger and you'll soon be the number one speaker for what you do in a crowded marketplace.*

> *The way to gain a good reputation is to endeavour to be what you desire to appear.*
>
> **SOCRATES**

2. **Write!** *There's no way round this one. You've got to write as much as you can! Articles, blogs, books – all enhance your expertise. Magazines, trade journals, local, regional and national newspapers, association newsletters and websites all need great content to make them interesting. Where are you and your thoughts/opinions/insights appearing in written format?*

   Writing pre-sells others on your abilities, and exposes you to thousands of prospects. The word 'author' has the same root as 'authority' - you are the source! There's nothing quite like having your name in print to differentiate you from others that do what you do and give you that extra level of respect. You'll gain kudos from people that already know you and you'll gain attention from people that don't yet know you. Both avenues are vital in building your reputation as the number one 'go to' choice for what you do.

3. **Stay Current!** *It has been said that where you end up five years from now will depend on the people you've got around you and the books you've read. If you're not reading and learning, you're going backwards in today's fast-paced world. Investing in yourself will increase your knowledge, your expertise and your skills. People will seek you out because you know stuff and because you'll know where to find stuff.*

   Keep current in your field. Subscribe to e-mail newsletters, blogs, news feeds and specialised publications. This keeps you ahead of the game and starts to earmark you as an expert. When you start thinking about what you're keeping current with, you become a thought leader! Listen to podcasts and tune into webinars and teleseminars. Use mobile apps and gadgets. These deliver very up-to-date information. You must develop personally and professionally to cultivate and maintain your reputation. Develop a good professional development library. Look for books that address your industry, niche, and type of work.

   Invest in your skills, your stage craft and your marketing abilities. In this fast-moving world, skills can become obsolete quite quickly. Skill is the ability to do something well. The stuff you were doing a few years ago might be irrelevant today. The things you knew five years ago might be holding you back right now. The need to stay fresh and right up to date with your skill is vital for success in business today. Your continuing education should be life-long to keep you ahead of the chasing pack. Along with all of the top speakers, I invest at least 10% of my annual income back into professional development. You can get stuff in a one hour seminar with an expert that's taken them a lifetime to learn. That's got to be a great use of your time!

Attend conferences, conventions, trade shows, expos and exhibitions. By picking out half a dozen key business events over a twelvemonth period, you can keep yourself connected to all the people, knowledge and trends you need to be held in high repute.

You need to upskill and stay ahead of the game. Without the right skills, your ability to develop the reputation you want may be severely hindered. Even simple things like teaching yourself to touch type or mastering some new technology might mean you don't get left behind. As an example, to master the basics of a new language, you need to learn a vocabulary of around 2500 of the most frequently-used words. If you break that down to 3 new words a day for a couple of years, it's doable, right?

Whether it's understanding Twitter and Facebook, mastering your cell phone, building your networking skills or memorising some power scripts - upskill now! Your reputation will be so enhanced!

> ❝*I am always doing that which I cannot do, in order that I may learn how to do it.*❞
>
> **PABLO PICASSO**

4. **Speak More!** *This one sounds a bit crazy, as you are already a speaker. But speaking is the single biggest marketing strategy you can utilise to raise your profile, build your reputation and create more opportunities. Presenting and speaking sets you up as the authority. You leverage your time and your impact as you're reaching out to many people at the same time. Whether it's to small*

audiences and meetings, or larger conferences and seminars, actively search out and fill opportunities to address an audience.

If you really want to build your speaking reputation quickly and emphatically, go out and speak more! Find an audience, craft a compelling message and address them with your insight and passion. That may mean conquering your fear of speaking, but there are lots of great teachers and trainers who will help you with your presenting. Ask me and I'll introduce you to my top three!

5. **Network Strategically!** *As somebody who spends his life teaching people how to be world class networkers, you can take it from me that this is THE business skill you have to learn if you want to be successful in life. Without it, you'll be isolated, out of touch, disconnected and relationally bankrupt! Along with speaking and writing, networking is the best thing you can do to build your reputation*

Your network is who you know. Your reputation is who knows you. Build your reputation by association by getting around the right people. The best reputations in the world can be undermined by ill-chosen connections and poorly-managed relationships. People will judge you by the people you hang around with. Ensure those people fit with your desired reputation!

21st century networking involves social media and online platforms such as Facebook, Twitter, YouTube and LinkedIn. Blending your offline face to face networking and the online connecting is the savvy way to raise your profile, build strong partnerships and share your content.

Forming strategic alliances is crucial to your success. Find other companies and individuals that you can work with that share the same market without directly competing with you. Do joint ventures and contra deals. Set up key partnerships. Source new introducers, customers and clients.

I have the privilege of heading up the Global Networking Council **www.globalnetworkingcouncil.com**. *As part of my GNC role, I interview the world's top thought-leaders, authors and experts on topics such as networking, referrals, influence, word of mouth, relationship capital, trust and presence.We put these interviews up on the GNC website where you can download them or listen, for FREE! One thing that comes out is that networking is not a one off event but a long term process. Networking never sleeps. It's a never ending sequence of connecting, meeting, talking and listening. It's something you do every day.*

You build your reputation and your network one relationship at a time, one conversation at a time. The world's most successful people follow the rule of 'Know and Be Known!'

> **"***Tell me what company you keep and I'll tell you what you are.***"**
>
> **MIGUEL DE CERVANTES**

Become the Expert and Build Your Reputation

If you want to stand out in any field, you need to be the perceived expert. An expert is a person who has a comprehensive and authoritative knowledge of or skill in a particular area. Wikipedia tells us that an expert is someone widely recognized as a reliable source of technique or skill. A person with extensive knowledge or ability based on research, experience, or occupation and in a particular area of study.

Words such as specialist, guru, connoisseur, master... all apply to a person who seems to know more than everyone else on a particular topic. The more you become known as a source of expert information, the more potential clients will trust you. And the more interesting people and influential contacts will be drawn to you. You can become an expert by virtue of your credentials, training, education, professional qualifications, publications or experience. Experts have special knowledge of a subject beyond that of the average person even to the point where it can be relied on legally.

Somebody once said that while the novice sees many possible explanations and options, the expert sees few. Experts use their knowledge to achieve performance that mortals like us assume requires extreme or extraordinary ability! They are faster, more accurate and more insightful. Experts are thought leaders and centres of influence. People like to do work with people they know, or know of. Experts ease that choice. Experts are not just clever or smart. Absent minded professors might know quantum physics but might be clueless about how to make a cup of tea.

Experts have a knack for insight. They apply their knowledge to solve your problems. Sometimes their insight allows them to define a problem that you cannot see or articulate. This is because they go so deep with their domain. Here are a few amusing yet thought provoking quotations on experts:

> *My definition of an expert in any field is a person who knows enough about what's really going on to be scared.*
>
> **P. J. PLAUGER**

Whatever it is with experts, there's something about them that draws others to them. They feature in conversations. They see things differently to us mortals. People revere and defer to them. Experts have an aura about them that says they simply know or can do more. They solve problems from a different starting point to the rest of us. Their insight and perception is on a whole different level to the rest of us. They are wiser and think more deeply about 'stuff.'

Experts are world-class. They rank the best of the best. They have an international standard of excellence that shadows pretty much everyone else. Every industry, profession, domain or topic has its experts. These people stand out as influencers, thought leaders and the ones that everyone else follows. So while you might be a speaker, what must you do to become any kind of an expert who speaks? Here are five tips:

1. **Pick a niche.** *You can't be all-knowing or brilliantly skilful with everything. You have to choose a topic, a subject area, a particular audience. Perhaps even a micro-nice, which is a niche within a niche. You can dominate a niche by being THEIR expert, better than you can be ANYBODY's expert. When you pick a niche, you can dominate a smaller, more focused community of dedicated followers, fans and admirers. You'll know their problems, their challenges, their thoughts and feelings and their world. That puts you in a powerful position as the number one 'go to' choice for what you do. There are very few really successful generalists these days. When it comes to building a world class reputation, the specialist is king!*

2. **Practice diligently.** *In his book Outliers, Malcolm Gladwell stated that the top performers in any field have invested more than 10,000 hours into their craft to become world class. At 1000 hours a year, or 20 hours a week or 3-4 hours a day, that's a 10 year slog. That's why it makes me laugh that people call themselves social media or business networking experts after being in the game a few short months!*

3. **Say 'No'.** *Experts appreciate the 'opportunity cost' of their expertise. You can't be brilliant at everything. You just say no to some stuff, which is what frees you up to go deeper with your chosen field. John Maxwell puts it well: "Say 'no' to the good so you can say 'yes' to the great."*

4. **Get published.** *The power of writing a book is huge! Getting your name in print is one of the most powerful things you can do to set yourself apart as an expert. This is not for commercial reasons, but for positioning reasons. Author = authority!*

5. **Spread the word.** *It's no good being a secret expert! People need to know how brilliant you are. Otherwise you're just some sad genius in a dark room keeping your gifts and your huge brain to yourself!*

So expertise = reputation. And hopefully you're now more knowledgeable about what it means to be that expert who speaks. And it's who you become in the eyes of others as the expert and number one authority for what you do. Above all, be authentic. Be you. That's real and that's compelling.

> *Always be a first-rate version of yourself, instead of a second-rate version of somebody else.*
>
> **JUDY GARLAND**

So there you have it. Five brilliant reputation building tips and strategies to help make you the number one, compelling, obvious, stand out choice for whatever it is that you do. I coach speakers to build more successful speaking businesses, forge 'stand out' reputations and make more money. If I can help you further in these areas, please get in touch at **www.therobbrown.com**

> *A good reputation will get all the right people saying all the right things behind your back!*
>
> **ROB BROWN**

ROB BROWN *FPSA*

Rob Brown is a global authority on building and leveraging powerful networks. A bestselling author of *How to Build Your Reputation* and an in-demand conference speaker, he works with leaders, entrepreneurs and senior executives who are great at what they do BUT want to 'stand out' more and sell themselves, their ideas and their 'stuff' much better. He shows them how to become powerfully CONNECTED, extremely VALUABLE and highly VISIBLE with all the right people. As a result, they soon become the compelling 'go to' choice and influential 'player' in their space, with all the kudos, wealth and opportunities that brings. A regular media contributor and thought leader around collaborative workforces and connected employees, Rob's clients include HSBC, RBS, Deloitte and GE. His popular newsletter, *The Connected Professional*, contains high level networking nuggets, reputation building insight and career acceleration tips, and goes out to thousands of people each week.

Connect to Rob on

EMAIL: *rob@rob-brown.com*

PHONE: *+44 (0) 115 846 2127*

WEBSITE: *www.therobbrown.com*

TWITTER: *@therobbrown*

LINKEDIN: *www.linkedin.com/in/therobbrown*

FACEBOOK: *www.facebook.com/therobbrown*

YOUTUBE: *www.youtube.com/gotochoice*

CHAPTER TWO

A Speaker Has No Business without Sales and Marketing

MIKE PAGAN *MPSA*

Don't swear at me, I'm not a salesman, I do business development! So many people have issues with the phrases "Business Development", "Sales" and "Marketing". Apply these to the business of professional speaking and it gets even harder. I have tried numerous business development techniques and activities with varying results, some successes; others complete failures and a waste of time and money. My interpretation of these three phrases is relatively simple:

Business Development is the overriding umbrella where all activities within the sales and marketing arena sit – simple.

Everyone is in Sales to a greater or lesser extent; it is purely the creation of a deal to exchange goods or services in exchange for cash or cash equivalent. Many people don't believe or don't want to believe that they are in Sales and shy away from anything vaguely sales related as it is perceived as dirty or vulgar.

Marketing is the simple art of manifesting a situation where an opportunity to influence can occur – the Sale. Marketing can range from being very creative and arty through to the more logical practices of market research and data analysis.

If Marketing is simply the action required to get you into a situation with a potential buyer, then that doesn't sound too difficult to me. If only it were that easy. The big problem is that within the speaking world there are hundreds and thousands of experts, all claiming to have the magic solution in a (perceived) similar field of expertise to you. Demonstrating your uniqueness and credibility is just one challenge of marketing; the other is being seen and heard.

What are your options?

Consider this list of marketing activities - you could act upon any one of them right now to increase the number of meetings needed for you to sell:

Networking, Social media (Facebook, Twitter, Blogging, podcasting, LinkedIn, Pinterest, Google+, metatags etc. etc.), speaking, showcases, conferences, exhibitions, websites, direct marketing, emails, webinars, market research, forums, advertising (paper, radio, billboards, TV, pay-per-click, advertorials, affiliate programmes, SEO etc. etc.), door to door, cold calling, newsletters, databases (past, current, dormant, one-off, key influencers, fans, friends, family).

This list is far from exhaustive and to make things harder most professional speakers do not have the luxury of a large team backing them with business systems such as financial management, budgets and marketing plans. So something has to give – an SME, a speaking business or a start-up all have to focus on quality, not quantity. Marketing agencies will provide evidence that every one of these marketing activities can and will work for your business – however the challenge is that none of us have an endless pot of cash, time or energy that we can throw at it. So we have to choose.

Consider the difference between above the line marketing - i.e. activities you pay for directly or below the line where at minimal or no cost you create the groundswell of noise and activity to support you and build awareness and knowledge of who you are and what you do. Below the line marketing is the area where you should concentrate your efforts. Examples for demonstrating your expertise and knowledge in this way would be by writing articles, white papers, books and blogging and getting them online or printed.

What are the Quick Wins?

Quick wins have never worked for me. A classic example would be the time I threw money at a telesales firm to create some appointments for me. Initially they had to develop a data list of event companies to approach on my behalf, make the connection at the 1st, 2nd or 3rd attempt, send on information, follow up to confirm receipt and then be told ..... "We've put Mike's details on file, thank you". Sadly I can report that this was a resounding failure for me. Poor data, not enough commitment given, more cash required to extend the trial - all of the above.

Free Costs, How Much?

Most people focus in on the "free" i.e. no-costs activities, those that do not incur huge outlays of cash. Before I hear you shouting at me, I know there is no such thing as "free", allow me to demonstrate – if you take 5 hours every week on any one activity that is a huge investment in time, resource and energy.

Take for example the one giant time drain that so many speakers use - "social media". Following the example of 5 hours per week (a very conservative estimate on a five day working week) this equates to 250 working hours per year – that equates to over 6 weeks of employed work if you still had a boss and salary. The tough question here is do you honestly understand where all of your time goes? Use a FAFFometer® or an equivalent time sheet on yourself (free versions are available at **www. mikepagan.com**).

Many speakers would say that is a fair price to pay, but there are some speakers who will hit the dizzy heights of 3-5 hours per day on social media - 750-1250 hours per year - 18-30 working weeks per year!! Now it might not cost in cash transactions but it does still cost you. Don't get me wrong, social media does work, but if like me you are non-techie and fail to get overly excited by the idea of sitting for long periods of time in front of a keyboard, then you have to be creative: outsource it, use clever contra-deals or find joint ventures with others to do it all or part of it for you - it's your choice, it is your business after all.

If you can't measure it, then you can't do it!

Clearly everything adds up, so pick 5-6 marketing channels, commit to them fully and monitor and measure them all the time. According to the rules of business or marketing if you can't measure it or track it then you can't do it! I certainly agree with that statement, even if like many people I fail to adhere to it at all times.

Measuring enables you to take an impersonal, holistic view of what activities are taking place and what works, providing very visual evidence of progress. By measuring activities and outputs, longer term trends become visible - seasonal changes, buying cycles of top clients, peaks and troughs in cashflow to name but a few.

A simple process for you to consider using is the tracking of proactive approaches on the telephone. A daily target is set that must be achieved; failure to do so will mean a rollover onto the next day's target. For example, if the target was 5 calls per day (equating to 1200 per annum on a 48 week year!) and only 2 are achieved, then the following day's target would be 8. However if you have a great day today making 10 calls, the target is still to do 5 tomorrow, no banking is allowed, this is developing a positive habit. Take an average month of 22 working days and that equates to a minimum target of 110 proactive approaches. How many appointments and meetings can be generated by that volume of proactivity? Then calculate your conversion rate from first visit to agreed sale and multiply that across the year, interesting reading!

The main point is this – without a history of where you have been or what you have achieved how will you truly understand what does and doesn't work? Knowing at the end of every year where your successes have come from and what has generated the most business for you will enable you to sit back, reflect and plan for the following year with a strangely smug glow about you.

There is one sales approach that has not worked for me or any other speaker I know so I recommend caution here. There are web companies offering to promote all the best speakers from all over the world with promises such as 'for this week only you can get listings here, here, here and here and loads of leads and opportunities that all our 'A' listed speakers get for just XXXX investment' etc. If these guys call you, run away, I have not seen evidence of any successful relationships here.

To manage or not to manage?

No discussion about marketing would be complete without mentioning Bureaus and Agencies. I'll be honest, for me they do not work. I am not a celebrity speaker and therefore my name has little draw outside of the speaking world. Whilst I am on a number of books I have not received enquiries that have led to a reduction in my mortgage. However, I would say having a manager or management team is very important; this is the Business of Professional Speaking. Someone controlling your diary, your phones and your negotiations is a must as your business builds. In my previous corporate life I was negotiating fees that had little direct personal impact; win, lose or draw had no effect on my personal finances. I found it easy to do.

Your speaking fees can be increased dramatically by someone else negotiating on your behalf and removing that emotional connection to the fee. The management firm will contract for you, finalise the details, add your slightly strange personal clauses into the contract and tell you when the deal is done! A final caveat here - take your time, find where you fit, where you feel special rather than just a number. Your management team will not feed you all your business, they're not an agency but they will make you look far more professional, which will be reflected directly in your fees.

Rejection is part of life – deal with it.

I believe one of the speaker's greatest stumbling blocks is asking for the business, putting ourselves in the limelight and just asking. You need to remove the old-fashioned association of Sales with the timeshare rep or double-glazing salesman and see Sales as simply the art of communication, influencing another person to do your bidding. Personally it's no different to persuading friends to go to the pub rather than the cinema, or you suggesting your wife looks better in the red dress rather than the lime green one. It's not a big deal; it's about persuasion and having a good reason as to why someone should use your services. Without some persuasive communication everything grinds to a halt.

Remember nobody likes hearing that phrase on the phone, 'We'll put your information on file' or 'We've gone with xxx.' Rejection has always hurt; from the day when as a child you were told 'no' to doing something. Sales is a numbers game and only those that are willing to go the distance and persevere will be successful. In this brutal world of business development you might have to deal with 45 rejections before you get an opportunity, maybe more. Out of interest, have you made direct contact in the last week with 45 conference organisers, event companies or meeting planners? Just asking. There are those who appear more capable of taking knockbacks than others, those with 'thicker skin' who don't appear to take it personally when someone turns them down. Believe me, rejection hurts everyone. Sales is all about asking, if you never ask you will never get an answer!

What next?

What should you do next? Stop FAFFing about on random marketing and sales activities and cut back to five or six that you will truly commit to. You only have a finite amount of time, resources and cash, so spend each of them wisely. Measure and track every activity that you have committed to and then continuously review the good, the bad and the "could do better". You are a business, and all businesses require sales, marketing, IT, admin and finance. Choose which parts you need to outsource - the things you are not very good at or the things you really don't like - trust me, you'll always put them off. Consider changing your mental approach and beliefs regarding sales and marketing by developing a team around you that will work together on your business development supporting you in your quest to succeed in the Business of Professional Speaking.

MIKE PAGAN *MPSA*

Mike Pagan is a highly recommended Motivational Speaker, Master of Ceremonies and author; he has a refreshingly different approach to productivity and time management, enabling people to access higher levels of success with the same resources as everyone else.

The Verb FAFF stands for the False Art of Feeling Fulfilled. Mike will challenge you to Stop FAFFing about doing things that are below your pay grade and focus on the areas that truly matter.

Time and productivity are the main casualties of FAFFing about, be that personally or professionally. We spend and waste money, time and effort FAFFing about on randomly selected activities that, at best, keep us busy.

As the Master of Ceremonies Mike has a primary objective - to make the event memorable for all the right reasons. This is achieved through balancing his ability to provide strong and powerful business links between speakers, themes and objectives for the event.

EMAIL: *speaking@mikepagan.com*

PHONE: *+ 4 419 2645 0090*

WEBSITES: *www.mikepagan.com*
www.stopfaffingabout.com
www.breakingfrontiers.com

LINKEDIN: *www.linkedin.com/in/mikepagan*

TWITTER: *@mike_pagan*

FACEBOOK: *www.facebook.com/pages/Mike-Pagan-Speaker/119417171462473*

YOUTUBE: *www.youtube.com/user/mikepagan*

GOOGLE: +: *www.plus.google.com/102149414198705223435/posts*

CHAPTER THREE

How to Profit from Finding out What Your Client Really Wants

SIMON HAZELDINE *MPSA*

You receive an enquiry from a possible client who may wish to book you to speak at their event, or you meet someone who could be a suitable client for you at a networking event.

In this situation far too many speakers fall into the trap of immediately talking about themselves and what they speak about. The potential client finds himself on the receiving end of a well-intended and very passionate "sales pitch" that despite your best intentions is probably going to fail.

Most of us have had the experience of being talked "at" by a salesperson. The salesperson literally bombards you with information in the hope that this is going to persuade you to make a purchase. With little or no idea of what you are interested in, they carpet bomb you with information and hope that some of it hits home. This is sometimes called the "spray and pray" sales technique and is not recommended for professional speakers who want to get booked!

At the very early stages of any interaction with a potential client your focus should be on gaining a good understanding of the client, the context or circumstances of their situation, their needs, goals, challenges and problems.

Once you have done this then (and only then) you can use what you have discovered as a catalyst to motivate the client to take action and to book you!

In the same way that a medical doctor will not prescribe treatment until he has diagnosed the patient's symptoms, it is vitally important to diagnose the client's problems before offering any form of solution. And your speech needs to offer at least some sort of solution to their problems.

Quite often your initial contact may come from the conference organiser, a secretary, PA or perhaps a bureau who has been tasked with securing a suitable speaker. As important as these people are, it is very important that you get access to the key stakeholder. You need to get access to the most senior manager or leader of the organisation in question that has a stake in the success of the conference. Quite often this will be someone like the Managing Director, CEO or a Vice President.

I always ask to be connected to this person and explain that I want to make certain that I am the right speaker for the event and to make sure that my message will meet the client's needs and will fully support the aims of the conference.

I will probably not be able to get this sort of information from the person who initially makes contact, and if I don't get access to the key stakeholder I will miss out on other opportunities for me that may exist in the client's business.

Once I have gained access to the senior person (either face to face or over the 'phone) then I will use the following questioning process that I have found to be very effective:

1. **Current Situation.** *Where is the client now? Question the client to get a full understanding of their current situation. You may wish to question them about the market they operate in, their competitors, their people, their strategy and what they are hoping to achieve in the future, current initiatives and projects, how they see their business changing and so forth. The aim of this stage is to develop a good understanding of their business.*

2. **Past Situation.** *What has happened in the past? It is helpful to understand the client's previous circumstances particularly if what has happened in the past has contributed to, or is the cause of the current situation. It can also be useful to understand the client's personal or career history as a way of furthering rapport with them and developing a deeper understanding of their experience (which may shape their buying approach) and to identify factors that may affect the criteria they will use to make a buying decision.*

3. **Problems and Pain.** *Where are they hurting? What problems and challenges is the client facing? What isn't working as it should? What opportunities are being missed? Who or what is not performing to the required standard? What frustrations does the client have? It is important also to ask questions to begin to make the client fully aware of what this is costing them.*

   This can include:

   Financial cost – how much is the current problem costing them? All businesses are interested in reducing cost as a way of making more profit. Where is the client wasting money? Where are they losing money? Where are they missing out on opportunities to make additional money?

Strategic cost – where is the problem impacting on the client's strategic aims? For example, if they want to expand their business, how is the problem preventing them from doing that?

Personal / emotional cost – What impact does the problem have on the client. Is it making them or their employees angry and frustrated? Is it wasting their time? Does the client or their employees have to work longer hours because of the problem? Does it make their life more complicated and challenging?

The aim of the questioning is to make the client fully aware of the "painful" impact the problem is having. You are making the client aware of the real, genuine cost and impact of the problem. You are raising their awareness of the cost of the problem(s) they are facing.

4. **Goal / Future Situation.** *What does the client want to achieve? Ask questions to elicit their desired outcome. Ask questions about what a successful resolution to the problem would look like and what benefits it would bring them. Be aware that they may not always be able to fully articulate this, and in helping them to become clear about what they want to achieve, you will again have been of good service and value to them.*

5. **Negative Impact.** *So far we have made sure we understand the client's situation, we understand their history and what has led up to their current situation. We have explored the problems they are experiencing and the pain these are causing and we have determined a goal or future situation where the problem has been solved.*

We need to make them reflect upon and consider the impact and costs associated with this. In Step 3 we began to stir the financial, strategic, personal and emotional pain. In Step 5 we must increase the client's perception of the pain they will experience if they do not take action.

Sometimes one of the strongest competitors you will face is the client deciding to "do nothing", where the client decides to pause and procrastinate. They will only do this if the pain that they perceive is not strong enough or the reward they will receive is not compelling enough.

So make sure this is not going to happen! Ask questions to help your client understand the full implications of not taking action. What will be the costs, particularly the financial costs of not taking action? What will happen if the current circumstance remains?

It can be helpful to get them to consider the short, medium and longer term consequences of the problem to motivate them to take action. It is important to monetise the pain so that you can provide great clarity to the client about what the problem is costing them. They need to see this and feel this.

6. **Positive Impact.** *You now need to add some positive motivation. In the same way that you have extrapolated the short, medium and long term pain impact, now do the same by showing the client the benefits they can expect to receive once the problem has been solved.*

   This can of course be a simple as reversing the loss or pain impact. Demonstrating and emphasising the reward in this way will also help further on in the sales process when you discuss the price of your services.

When you have followed this process you should have a situation where you and the client have a shared understanding of their problems and challenges including any financial impact. You have painted a picture of a future situation where these problems have been removed and the client is benefitting. With this knowledge you can now position how what you have to offer will meet their needs, help to solve their problems and gain the benefits from this.

"Hang on!" I can hear you saying. "This seems like a lot of effort to go to for one booking! Do I really have to go to all this trouble?"

The simple answer is no, you don't. If you are comfortable missing out on extra business and revenue then you don't need to bother with this process. However, if you are interested in gaining multiple pieces of business from one client then this process is a must.

Let me give you an example of how I have used this process and the benefits gained.

I received a phone call from the PA of the Managing Director of the UK division of a global company. The Managing Director had read one of my books (books often lead to speaking engagements as you will see in the next chapter!) and was interested in booking me to speak at their forthcoming national sales conference.

The PA asked for my availability for the date in question and my fee. I replied that I could possibly be available on the date in question but would need to check and confirm (the more scarce you are, the more people value you!) and that I would need to meet with the Managing Director to understand what he was looking for before being able to confirm my fee. I explained that I wanted to make 100% certain that I was the right speaker for their conference and that I wanted to fully understand their aims and objectives. I agreed a date with the

PA to meet the Managing Director in person which is always my preferred option.

I met the Managing Director and after some initial small talk asked him what he wanted to gain from the conference, what themes were included and why these themes were important before moving into the questioning process I outlined above.

A key problem that I uncovered was that the sales force was not productive enough. They were struggling to balance time and effort with results. They did not have enough discipline in following a proven sales process and as a result they were not securing enough appointments per day which in turn was leading to lost revenue. I calculated the revenue that was being lost with the Managing Director and what revenue increase could be expected should the situation improve.

I said that I thought I would be able to help and the Managing Director then asked me what my speaking fee was. I quoted my full fee and he agreed without question - although to be honest he did seem to wince a little bit! Due to the conversation we had had about the revenue they were currently missing out on, by comparison my fee seemed more acceptable.

We then had a conversation about other possible ways that I could be of assistance to their organisation. And to make a long story short here is the business that has resulted to date:

1. *Keynote speech at sales conference*

2. *Follow on consultancy working with senior sales leadership team to devise a structured sales process and sales call methodology*

3. *Training sales management team to coach and develop their sales people to implement the new sales process*

4. *Training the entire sales force in the new sales process*

5. *A bonus invitation to speak at the company's global "Elite Client" conference in Monaco. The night before the conference I was invited to have dinner with several of the company's elite clients where I discussed their business challenges with them. This resulted in two additional speaking gigs*

Most keynote speakers that I know tell me that they provide additional services such as consultancy, training and coaching to their clients. Spending the time necessary to really understand a client's business will uncover numerous opportunities for you to add value to your relationship with them which, will in turn, add money into your bank account.

SIMON HAZELDINE *MPSA*

Simon Hazeldine works internationally as a professional speaker, performance consultant and corporate trainer in the areas of sales, negotiation, performance leadership and applied neuroscience.

His focus is on inspiring and enabling exceptional performance and delivering improved bottom line results for his clients.

Simon is the bestselling author of five books: *Bare Knuckle Selling, Bare Knuckle Negotiating, Bare Knuckle Customer Service, The Inner Winner* and *Neuro–Sell: How Neuroscience Can Power Your Sales Success.*

He has a Masters Degree in Psychology, is a Fellow of the Institute of Sales & Marketing Management, a longstanding member of the Professional Speaking Association and a licensed PRISM Neuroscience Brain Mapping Practitioner.

Simon is also the co-founder of www.sellciusonline.com – the leading on-line resource for sales professionals.

Simon's client list includes Fortune 500 and FTSE 100 companies and as a highly experienced and in-demand international speaker he has spoken in over 30 countries across six continents.

EMAIL: *simon@simonhazeldine.com*

PHONE: *+44 (0) 1509 416 942*

WEBSITES: *www.simonhazeldine.com*
www.neuro-sell.com

TWITTER: *@simonhazeldine*

CHAPTER FOUR

Use Your Books to Get Booked and Earn More

MINDY GIBBINS-KLEIN *FPSA*

"Every speaker needs to have a book." I hear that everywhere I go, and you may have heard people say it too. Several things are true about this statement:

- *Speakers with books have more credibility*
- *Speakers with books tend to get higher fees*
- *For many meeting planners, speakers must be published authors to even be considered for the gig*

Let's take a quick look at why the above statements are true. Put yourself in the shoes of a meeting planner or client. You have two speakers in mind for a particular presentation. One of the speakers is a prolific author, having published one or two books, which you have seen around and heard people talking about online. You may have even read the book/s. That speaker is probably also blogging and writing articles pertinent to the book, enhancing the message and sharing it more widely.

The other speaker has not published any books. They sound good and they may blog or do videos regularly, but there is no book out there in the market to represent them. Be honest. Wouldn't you be more impressed and feel more confident about the speaker with a book? I have heard numerous stories of people getting the business because of their book. In one case, a client of mine lost an opportunity to another client of mine because 'the other guy seemed like he really knows his stuff; he has written a book".

It does give confidence to meeting planners, and in many cases it is almost a requirement. The application forms for many conferences used to say 'Have you written a book?' Now, not only do they assume you have a book in print, they ask you to list *all* your books!

The growth and ease of self-publishing and the general trend for people to believe they are experts have led to a situation where there are over one million books being published each year, and that number is growing all the time. If you add ebooks to the mix, we are talking millions and millions. So, simply having a book is not as rare or special as it used to be, and it has become table stakes: the bare minimum you need to play the game.

What Kind of Book do *You* Want to Have?

If you have published a full-length book in print, you will know the feeling of seeing and touching that book for the first time. You probably saw the brown box and felt a feeling of excitement and anticipation build in your body. Then, opening the box and taking the book out, perhaps you looked at it in awe, thinking 'Did I really produce this?' The feeling of bringing a book into the world has been likened to the feeling of having a baby (including the labour pains!), which is why I called my company and methodology The Book Midwife®. And similar to a child, the book will live on and be your legacy.

It is a real achievement to write a book, and 95% of all the people who say they want to and are going to write a book, never do it. So, simply writing and publishing a book is a big achievement, and don't let anyone try to take away your feeling of pride, satisfaction and personal fulfilment. However, as I mentioned above, the value of a book has diminished or at least been diluted by the large number of sub-standard documents masquerading as books, and the impact is not quite as strong as it used to be.

If you want to be a savvy speaker, you will need a great book, and you will use that book strategically to get booked more often, and earn more. Here are the ways savvy speakers use their books.

Before the Gig

When planning and writing your book, you really need to be sure about what you are developing. You may consider your book to be a high-end business card, as some people refer to business books, but I would encourage you to think of it with a bit more respect than that. The book is going to be representing you out there in the market. Many people who read the book may never get to meet you face-to-face. Therefore, it has to be good. As mentioned above, there are so many books being published that it is no longer a big deal to have a book. The bar has been raised, and the differentiator is now quality.

You need to have a good book. I call this your 'flagship book'. This is the book you are known for, and in many cases, people know the book but can't remember your name. That's OK! They can always Google the book and find you. When you have a good quality flagship book in the market, people start talking about the ideas you present in the book, and your reach and reputation will grow.

Recently, three different clients of mine had new client work from people who read their books, which convinced them they just *had* to work with the author personally. In two of these cases, it was a client from another country, and it is unlikely they would have connected if it hadn't been for the book.

So it is not just about having a book with your name on it. It must have new and exciting insights, models and ideas in it, to propel you into the big opportunities and get people talking about you.

A good book is one that contains your main message and puts it across in a way that the reader can grasp it, and it also is the right length, providing the right amount of depth to give people confidence that you know your subject inside-out. Unfortunately, the ease of publishing has led to a large number of ebooks and printed books that I would not even call a book. I have seen people promoting 37-page ebooks which really should be called 'special reports' and thin books that could be called 'booklets'. I do wonder how some people can present their 'books' with a straight face.

So what is the minimum length for a book? Well, this is a tricky question, and one that I get asked on a weekly basis by clients and audiences. My personal view is that, to contain enough good content and go into the depth I was speaking about earlier, your book needs to have at least 120 pages, or 25,000 words. Now, this is a big assumption, and a book can be padded out to 120 pages, or be filled with nonsense and fluff to reach a higher word count. So it comes down to the amount of content and value in the book. There is only so much you can do and tell with 5000 words (which someone told me is an acceptable word count for a book. I agreed to disagree with her.)

Equally, there is no need to produce a 400-page tome which is daunting to look at, much less lug around and read. You will never be able to put everything you know into your book, so you want to choose the right scope to give people a really good taste of your material, but not too much.

There is no way to cheat on your book. The reader is going to assess it according to his or her own standards and decide if it looks the part, feels the part and adds value.

You can and should have other thought leadership materials in the market as well as your book. Successful speakers tend to have a range of products, including reports, white papers, blogs, videos and articles, as well as full-length, hard-hitting, thought-leading books. When I work with business leaders on their thought leadership strategy, we figure out all the content and messages first, then look at all the different ways of getting that content into the market. The book is at the hub of the entire plan, and the other products support it.

Booking the Gig

Successful speakers also bring their book into the briefing and negotiation conversations. They include the book in packages, so that each attendee or participant gets a copy of the book, eliminating the need to stand at the back of the room selling your books. On average, 10-15% of an audience will buy a copy of the speaker's book at the end of the presentation. Speakers tend to take too many copies of their books to the venue, and end up taking them home again. I have pre-sold my book into a number of opportunities, and so have many of my successful speaker friends.

Pre-selling the books, or including them in a package, also gives you the opportunity to earn more from that gig, especially if the fee being offered is not what you were hoping for or expecting.

Savvy speakers offer a special edition of their book for their clients. Obviously, this requires a bit of time and a cooperative publisher who will create the special cover with the client's logo, message from the CEO etc. I have produced some of these special books for our speaker clients, and they go a long way toward building loyalty, as well as impressing everyone who receives a copy. Typically, these editions do not have an ISBN and so they are not available for trade sales.

During the Gig

Have your book on display on the stage, and ideally a few copies. This adds colour and gets the book branding onto people's radars. They will be seeing the book while you are speaking, and it will create an association and a subtle urge for people to have their own copy of the book when you have finished. They want to take a piece of you home with them!

Hold your book up during your presentation, but get the balance right. I once attended a talk where the author held his book up for nearly the entire 15 minutes he was speaking, and it became very uncomfortable and embarrassing. You definitely want to show people the book, and be proud of it. Hold it firmly, and slightly higher than you normally would. Just under your chin is fine, and it allows everyone in the audience to see it clearly (as well as looking good in photographs and videos). Treat your book with respect. If you toss your book onto a table, that looks like it is not valuable and you don't care about it.

Give copies away to audience members who ask or answer questions. It acts as an incentive, and creates interaction and excitement. If someone at the back wins the book, get it to someone in the front row and have them send it back. This way, lots of people touch the book, creating that desire to buy that I was talking about earlier. Thanks to one of my mentors, Nigel Risner, for this tip which I think he said came from Shay McConnon! Anyway, I have used this technique successfully many times!

Hold a prize draw to encourage people to give you their business cards and build your list. Give one or more copies of the book away and announce it while people are still there. Better yet, do it from the stage and make the winner come up to receive his/her copy – generating more excitement and photo opportunities.

Think out of the box and try something wild and crazy with your book. I have seen speakers do some impressive things with their books, while on and off stage, such as signing the book onstage with a big marker pen, reading a random sentence or paragraph from the book, and even building towers with their books! If you want to be memorable, bring some creativity into your talk, as well as giving the book some exposure.

After the Gig

Ideally you want a book table at the back of the room at each event (unless you have pre-sold the books as we discussed above). Get others to man the table so you can meet and greet people in front of the table, pose for photos, etc. You can use your own staff, or members of the client's team. It can build trust and rapport when you get others involved, especially if you give each one of them a copy of your book as a thank you.

If you have an ebook version of your book, or a sample chapter, you may want to send a link to people who have registered, or indeed to the entire list of participants if appropriate. A book or good excerpt is more valuable than other follow-up items you might see speakers offering. People will appreciate it.

You also want to inspire people to help you spread the word, even before they have read the book. If you have done a great job with your presentation, the audience will be motivated to talk about you and your content. Get them to agree to tweet and blog about you, and review your book. Let them know you are always available for interviews and webinars. Getting their agreement in advance allows you to go back to them later and say 'Thank you for promising to review my book...'

Finally, remember that your book is not just for Christmas. That means once you have it, you want to remember to promote it and use it in your speaking business for the long term. Some people publish a book and then do very little with it. Those same people tend to ask me why nothing is happening with their book, why they are getting few sales and little business from it. For your book to work for you, you need to *work it*. Constantly be on the lookout for ways to use the book to build your profile and reputation, and to give people a taste of your wisdom before they meet you, work with you or book you.

I wish you the best of luck with every aspect of writing and publishing your book, and if you ever need my assistance with any of it, you know where to find me (curled up on the sofa reading a good book, or at my computer writing one!)

MINDY GIBBINS-KLEIN *FPSA*

Mindy Gibbins-Klein is founder and managing director of *REAL Thought Leaders, Panoma Press* and *The Book Midwife®*. She is a highly sought after speaker to executive audiences and top business leaders. She has spoken to and coached tens of thousands of people in 11 countries. Mindy is a Fellow of the PSA (Professional Speaking Association) and past president of the PSA London Region.

In addition to speaking, Ms Gibbins-Klein also maintains a small list of private consultancy clients who use her services to develop their writing, publishing and speaking strategy, and to plan, write and publish specific books and articles that raise their profiles as REAL thought leaders in the market.

Mindy has an enviable list of over 500 published clients, many of whom have received excellent media coverage and book sales. Mindy has written and been interviewed for articles, radio and television over 100 times on the subject of building a profile as a REAL thought leader, writing, publishing and speaking. She is also a regular columnist for several magazines and online publications, as well as being an expert consultant for several communities of business leaders. She is the author and co-author of seven books (including this one).

EMAIL: *mindy@mindygk.com*

PHONE: *+44 (0) 845 003 8848*

WEBSITE: *www.mindygk.com*

TWITTER: *@bookmidwife*

LINKEDIN: *www.linkedin.com/in/mindygibbinsklein*

CHAPTER FIVE

Getting Clients Should Be The Hard Bit - Keeping Them Should Be Easy

STUART HARRIS *MPSA*

A few years ago as I was speaking to a financial services client of mine, he told me that he was "great at attracting customers, but after a year or so, they left for another service provider". His situation was not unique in his industry or with many people in the speaking industry. Most of his focus was in attracting and acquiring new customers, with little attention placed on what he did with his customers once he got them.

As I discussed the situation further with my client, I identified that he had great acquisition plans to get his new customers, but very few retention strategies to keep them happy, content and to continue buying.

Unlike many speakers, trainers and coaches, he had a massive marketing and advertising budget at his disposal, however, what he did have in common with many of my colleagues was a fantastic online and offline presence.

Online, his company was very active on Twitter and Facebook; their website was fully optimised to inform potential customers about their fantastic product range, services available and promotional offers.

They were great at 'getting people in' from their very effective acquisition strategy, but had nothing in place to retain customers.

So, I sat down with him and we worked out a number of strategies, which would allow him to retain and grow his existing customer base as well as increase their spend.

We in the speaking, training and coaching world can all learn from this far from unique situation to help retain and develop our business and grow our average client spend.

Identify Your Client's Pain

As Simon mentioned in his excellent chapter, one of the first things to fully understand is the pain that your client goes through.

Many consultants visit potential and existing clients and tell them all of the things that they have to offer – they may have a portfolio including Communications Skills, Motivation & Inspiration Models, Sales Techniques, Networking Strategies, Management Principles, Creative Thinking Programmes etc., as well as a detailed list on how they can deliver it - Keynote Speeches, Training Workshops, 1-2-1 Coaching, Webinars, Books, Online Learning Programmes, etc.

They provide a lengthy list of what they do and how they do it and feel they have done their job properly if they leave their client with a comprehensive list of 'what is on offer'.

This, in the sales world, is known as "feature dumping", and is totally ineffective. Without fully analysing your clients' needs and understanding their "pain", you will never be in a position to tailor the most appropriate solution to meet those specific needs.

Before you can tailor your response to your client, you must understand what their needs are. This can only be done through thorough questioning to unearth the pain that the client is going through at that time.

Ask huge open questions, to make sure that the client does most of the talking. Whilst they're doing so you can be thinking "What will I ask next?" "Where am I going to take this conversation?"

Ask questions such as:

- *What has changed since the last time we met?*
- *What improvements are you looking to see after 'the event'?*
- *What are the toughest challenges that you are currently facing?*
- *What future problems do you anticipate?*
- *How will you know what good looks like?*
- *What happens if this isn't fixed/resolved?*

When you have a general overview of what your client's needs are, you need to probe further to help your client prioritise their problems. You can do this by asking **TED** questions:

- *TELL me more about XXX*
- *Could you EXPLAIN to me how this affects your business?*
- *Is it possible to DESCRIBE what will happen if this is not resolved?*

Try to get them to think of the long term repercussions if this problem is not resolved, not just the short-term pain. You may find that although a client has an immediate problem, there may be bigger underlying issues that you can help them with which will relieve them of greater complications and more damaging consequences further down the road.

Once you fully understand the pain that you and your client have jointly identified and prioritised, you can then tailor your solutions to meet their needs.

In sales, people talk about FABs – no it's nothing to do with Thunderbirds nor does it stand for Features And Benefits. It stands for Features, Advantages and Benefits.

- *Features – What a certain part of the product/service is.*
- *Advantage – What it does.*
- *Benefit – Why this product/service will be of benefit specifically to you, Mr Client.*

Wherever possible, tailor your response using their words when making your 'benefit statement', for example, "You said earlier on, Mr Client, that one of the problems you are facing just now is XXX and if you don't resolve that quickly you will YYY. Well, what I can do for you is ZZZ. Is that the sort of thing that could help you resolve this issue?"

Put yourself in your client's shoes, ask yourself the question "What's in it for them?" Why should they buy from you or continue to seek you out for your advice and support? Think about the long-term relationship, not just the one-off transaction.

One way to find out what the general pain is in a certain sector is to keep an eye on discussions in LinkedIn groups that are appropriate to your market place or niche. What questions are being asked? Could you offer some free advice or solutions? Do you have friends in that field that you could ask for additional advice?

Engage with your client the way THEY want to be engaged

How are you communicating with your clients?

You may send out newsletters, blog, utilise advanced CRM tools or just use a simple Excel spreadsheet to track client engagement activity. Some people just pick the phone up and call clients on an odd occasion.

You may well be interacting with your clients in one of the social media forums such as LinkedIn, Twitter, Facebook Business Pages, FourSquare, Google+, YouTube channels as well as interacting with them via 1-2-1 emails and webinars. The list of ways to engage with your clients is endless.

Many people nowadays shy away from the old traditions of 'Relationship Selling', where sellers would phone clients and take them out for a boozy lunch and pitch their wares when the client was half loaded, and had a cloudy head and a guilty conscience, so bought with delayed remorse.

However, if you have and are developing a genuine relationship with them, they may be happy to spend some time in your company over a coffee, a spot of lunch or even a quick breakfast meeting.

Very few, if any, connections with your client should include a sales pitch; make them feel special, wanted and cared for.

Send them website links that you've stumbled across or an article that you found in a magazine or trade journal with a brief note saying "I saw this and thought you might find it useful/ interesting" – no hard sell; it just lets them know that you have them on your mind.

Have you ever asked your clients how they would like you to communicate with them? Some of them may be too polite to say "Stop bombarding me with weekly newsletters, however, a catch up on the phone (or over a coffee) every month or so would be great".

I personally receive so many newsletters and 'must read bulletins' from one colleague of mine that I don't read ANY of them; however, if he called me once a month or met for a coffee I'd be much happier to find out what he's up to.

Are you ignoring your clients or killing them under a sea of newsletters, emails and Twitter/LinkedIn/Facebook posts or have you got the balance just right?

Recognise and Reward Loyalty

One of the reasons my insurance client was losing business was because when it came time to renew their policies, their customers started to shop around, even before their policy came to an end. The first time the company heard from them, since sending them their welcome letter, was on a report telling them which clients had left that month.

When his 'Winback Team' contacted them, the customer had already researched, chosen and signed up with a new provider – why should they stay loyal?

Brand disloyalty is huge these days – how many of us chop and change phone, credit card or utility suppliers just because we see promotional offers all over the television or internet for NEW CUSTOMERS.

What do you do to recognise your client's loyalty? Do you share best practice with them, send Christmas, birthday or Thank You cards, offer discounts for books or repeat work, provide free ebooks or online courses, advise on what is going on in their marketplace?

What are you doing to make it essential to have a relationship with you, as opposed to trying out someone else?

Profile Your Clients

Have you ever restricted the companies that you partner with because they are too difficult to work with, too time consuming for too little a reward, or their values just don't fit in with yours?

Take some time out and review where your business comes from. Are you relying too much on just a handful of clients or do you spread yourself too thinly across too many one-off customers? What happens if there is a change at the top or a refocus on priorities and they decide they no longer wish to use your services (no matter how good you are)?

Also, ask yourself "Is this organisation going to put into practice what I spoke to them about and will their leadership and management team reinforce my message?" If not, will they really see a return on their investment? If that is the case, in their eyes will that reflect badly on you or their organisation?

It's more likely than not that they will think that it was you who didn't deliver. Have you put some follow up strategy in place to help reinforce your message, or do you just walk away when the invoice has been paid?

Is your client willing to pay more for a very tailored speech or workshop specific to their needs and wants or are they looking for a low cost, slightly tweaked off-the-shelf solution? Are you charging a similar rate across all of your clients or are you working out a cost per event for each client or engagement?

Are you providing fillet steak service but only charging minced beef prices? Where are you investing your time and efforts and who really deserves your talents?

Learn From Your Mistakes

Many years ago I worked for Coca Cola. They were really focused on continuous development, so used a number of coaching models and structured development programmes for improvement. Many of the tools were very complex and contrived, therefore often ignored by managers.

However, my manager at the time, Robert Caley, had one very simple but extremely effective question that he would ask after each client visit – "what's your MLD?" I knew straight away that he wanted me to consider "What could I have done MORE of? What could I have done LESS of?" And most importantly, "If I had to do that client visit again, what would I do DIFFERENTLY next time?"

That was over 20 years ago, and I still use Robert's MLD model to this day. It stops me from being overly self-critical, but does identify ways in which I can improve on everything that I do.

Do you use a similar model or do you just skim through 'Happy Sheets' at the end of an event to determine whether you have done a good job or not – you should know better than anyone else whether you have done a good job or not.

Do you video yourself in action and play it back to determine what your MLD could be?

Upselling & Cross Selling

Upselling and Cross Selling are expressions that are bandied around a lot in sales. If you're not sure what upsell is, go into a fast food 'restaurant' and if they say "Do you want to go large on that?" that's upselling. If they say "Do you want a nuclear blasted hot apple pie with that?" that's cross-selling.

So, if you're doing a 'gig' for a client, is there something that you can do in addition to your speech or workshop or coaching session?

To Upsell your services, can you ...

- *Run an additional workshop in the afternoon?*
- *Coach managers on the topic that you've been delivering?*
- *Include copies of your book to create a higher value package deal?*
- *Sign people up to your newsletter for potential future sales?*
- *Sell in additional speaking events or training sessions (Buy One Get One Half Price?)*

To Cross-sell your services; can you ...

- *Present other topics that you specialise in at future events?*
- *Arrange an executive coaching programme for a later date?*
- *Sell other products at the back of the room?*

Niche Your Market

When I went out on my own, I had a fantastic first year. I ran training workshops and spoke at conferences for businesses in multi-media, financial services, telecoms, transport logistics, a low-cost airline, a whisky distillery and a couple of small bits of work from random organisations, such as the NHS and local & city councils. My market was "a mile wide but an inch deep".

The work I picked up was through a fantastic network of work colleagues, past and present. If I wanted to replicate that year, I would either have to rely on those contacts again, be very lucky or identify a niche market that I could focus my efforts on. Ideally, find a market that was "an inch wide and a mile deep".

Rather than trying to be 'all things to all men' I decided I had to identify my target audience. So what could be my niche market?

Throughout my career, I held various roles in sales and customer service, including 10 years in training and management roles in contact centres. The contact centre industry was perfect for me – I am now considered one of the industry's go-to-guys for speaking, training and coaching in sales, service and management.

I now have a very focused market and know exactly who to target. When I go onto Social Media forums, I know who and where to focus my energies. I can keep myself up to date with what's going on in my market and continue to develop my own skills in those areas.

Who are you marketing yourself to? What is your niche?

Keep Your Clients Close and Your Competition Closer

Whilst it is important to keep in touch with your clients on a regular basis and know what is going on in your niche market, it is also helpful to be aware of what you competition is up to. Not to imitate what they are doing but to identify changes in your marketplace, keep up to date with new techniques and technology and find out if there are new styles of delivery, engagement and marketing.

You certainly shouldn't plagiarise what they are doing but you can certainly be influenced, enlightened and educated by what they are doing – however, make what you do your own, don't be a pale imitation of someone else.

What are your clients up to? Where do they go? What are their interests? What is going on in their world? If they attend certain conferences, try to be there, even if just as a guest. Where do they congregate? Not just in the flesh but virtually, on social media.

LinkedIn is ideal for this. Think about the groups that your existing and potential clients are involved in (you can find this out on their profiles).

As the old saying goes "If you want to catch fish, fish where the fish are".

Finally, it is important to remember that it is important to remember there are two areas of focus in sales – The Acquisition AND Retention of clients, pay as much attention to keeping and building your client relationship as you do on trying to win new business.

STUART HARRIS *MPSA*

Stuart Harris has worked in Sales and Customer Service roles for over 20 years; initially as a salesman then as a sales manager and for the last 12 years as a keynote speaker, trainer and coach. In the last 15 years he has worked for and with a wide range of field sales teams and call/contact centres.

He works closely with clients to identify organizational and individual skill gaps and only then develops solutions to bridge those specific gaps. His main focus is blue chip contact centres although regularly works closely with SMEs of varying sizes, whether fully established or in their set-up & launch phases.

His philosophy is simple; either give his clients what they 'perceive they need', or better still, spend some time with those with performance issues, so that he can identify individual skill gaps and recommend a specific course of action or solution to their needs.

He speaks at conferences, events and 'after dinners' on a number of topics including leadership and management development, improving performance, maximising sales and improving customer service.

EMAIL: *info@thestuartharris.com*

TELEPHONE: *+44 (0) 7708 640 876*

WEBSITE: *www.thestuartharris.com*

TWITTER: *@thestuartharris*

LINKEDIN: *uk.linkedin.com/in/stuartharrisatdrive/*

FACEBOOK: *www.facebook.com/drivetraining*

YOUTUBE: *www.youtube.com/thestuartharris*

GOOGLE +: *www.gplus.to/thestuartharris*

PINTEREST: *www.pinterest.com/stuartharris411*

CHAPTER SIX

Inject your DNA to make your Speech Unforgettable

EILIDH MILNES *FPSA*

Perhaps it is self-evident, however it is elementary that to be a good speaker you need to speak with enthusiasm and project a confident stance and posture. You are after all your number one visual and you must make that first impression count.

Memorability is all about your DNA – your delivery style, knowing your niche and being your authentic self.

D = delivery

N = niche

A = authenticity

Look after not only your physical needs but your and emotional self prior to speaking. Be in the right frame of mind and mentally prepared. Each audience deserves you to pitch at your very best. Consider this mnemonic which I call the '5 Ps' i.e. preparation and planning, promise, perfect, performance.

Before you start, make a habit of learning the names of several participants. By referring to a delegate by name during your speech you honour them; similarly when you refer to the other speakers and organisers. However, allow for cultural differences and regional preferences. Your objective is to be inclusive. Do not embarrass anyone.

Just like a successful athlete have a simple warm-up routine before going on-stage. Personally, I talk myself into 'the zone'. I find a quiet space and vigorously 'punch-up' into the air; thrusting my fists at invisible punch-bag. After 20 punches, I programme my mind with positive self-talk, *'Whatever these people need to hear today Eilidh, let it come out of your mouth. You're going to be great girl!'* I smile... trust myself... and run on! Remember if you are asked to speak, the audience is on your side. They want you to do well. So have fun and serve them well and by using these tips and learn to control your controllables.

You have about 90 seconds to capture an audience. Outlining the business agenda or detailing the company's history since March 1937 will only serve to alienate your audience. You should have a choice of snappy, scripted and rehearsed openers. Practice them until you can self-replicate; able to recite them word for word, time and time again; yet make them sound new and fresh each time you stand to deliver.

Drama is everything... so is fun! When you arrive on the platform, stand for a few moments; let the audience anticipate your presentation or say something funny to relax them; if you can manage both that's even better. Let your humour shine.

The pause is probably the most under-used delivery technique. Often, nerves get the better of you and before you know it, you're speaking so fast your audience is finding it hard to keep up. A pause presents a rich opportunity to connect with your listeners and add drama to your message. Real power comes from allowing your listener to anticipate what's coming next. Pausing stimulates involvement. Watch this short video **http://www.eilidhmilnes.com/speaker-materials-masterclass-interview** - learn how by harnessing the power of the pause, one of my clients increased his presentation success rate by 50%! Now that is surely a serious incentive for silence.

A pause can completely change the meaning of what is being said. e.g. "You have two ears and one mouth... and they should be used... PAUSE... to eat"! Err... no... that was not the ending the audience expected to hear. This amuses them; confuses them, keeps them involved, makes them listen more carefully. "You have two ears and one mouth and they should be used in this proportion," is what they most likely expecting to be quoted i.e. we you listen twice as much as you talk. I believe I first heard this twist, a mental sorbet from my colleague and mastermind buddy, John Hotowka FPSA.

Create a warm, inviting and intriguing learning environment. Develop an engaging mindset and delivery style. Take your audience on a journey and set your talk plan within the first few minutes. Then they can relax and enjoy the talk as you reach your signposts. Although several techniques are available for keeping audiences on track, principal among them is the need to talk about something that's relevant to them. By awakening interest you can inform, educate and create impact.

Show passion! Pizzazz! Nothing is more tedious than a speaker going through the motions of a talk. If you are not excited by your material, why expect your delegates to appreciate your talk?

Before creating slides, I strongly recommend you read Nancy Duarte's book *Resonate*. To date, it is the best book on slide preparation that I have come across. Lee Jackson also mentions Nancy and a number of fantastic ideas in his chapter later in this book). *Resonate* was recommended to me by Chris Davidson, another of my PSA UKI colleagues. Nancy's company designs the slides for corporates such as Apple and people like Richard Branson. These endorsements say it all. In the book, Nancy explains about the importance of creating what she refers to as a 'spark-line' in any presentation. Read more in *Resonate* and in Lee Jackson's chapter, coming up soon.

Care about your audience. Put yourself in their position. If possible make them the 'hero of the day.' I have a slide which depicts classic heroes such as Nelson Mandela and Princess Diana. As the slide builds, it portrays firemen, soldiers, nurses and then headshots of everyday people. People just like you... people the audience can identify with... there are blank spaces for them to picture themselves and their personal heroes. In fact, I have my slides prepared professionally and consider it money well spent. My talents are to deliver the material, not technically create it. Of course, I can tweak and develop, but the master slides and themes are designed by an expert.

To keep your audience on-board, tell interesting, relevant and powerful stories. Stories add rhythm and pace. When linked to appropriate metaphors they are a memorable way to guide understanding. Stories punctuate your talk making it more enlightening and entertaining. A good tale will stay with your audience long after your presentation has finished; long after the statistics have been forgotten. Storytelling allows you to create an impact loop until you've worked through your material. Incorporate the 'rule of three' as I have done in the first sentence of this paragraph. Personal stories add authenticity. They let the audience 'see' who you really are e.g. I tell a Kling-on story.

You can also quote a testimonial to add credibility. Recently at BAE systems, one of the delegates made this comment on the feedback form, *"Thank you for your enlightening delivery... I can only personally describe one of your stories as the 'most important five minutes' of 2013...*" That story was about how our daughter overcame her lack of confidence and moved from the Kling-on to the Confidence Queen. Leave your DNA in your talk. Mark it out as yours; make it personal with indelible fingerprints and footprints.

Years ago during teacher training, we were taught about the importance of vocal variety. It is like an audio blood transfusion. Can you whisper? Use a phrase in a foreign language? Mime? All of these capture the imagination and attention of any listener. Using appropriate or quirky quotations make more mental picture boxes.

When moving or gesticulating on the stage, do so with purpose; practice your talk and plan where you will be standing to deliver each story and key point. Plant these areas in your memory as it will help you to recall your talk.

Having a conversation with your audience develops rapport. They love it. They feel engaged and involved. They connect when you are "in the moment". Use your smile, your tone and your eyes. Create an eye-contact plan, so that by the end of the presentation you have looked each member of the audience in the eye. When you are talking to larger numbers, chunk the auditorium into sections and make sure you address each area. I can still remember a fantastic American speaker that I heard ten years ago. She is called Sue Cappeln. Sue has the ability to make each person feel that she has come all the way from the States specifically speak to him/her. She does this by using her eyes. I constantly strive to emulate her style.

Communication is a two-way process, transmission and reception. I used to work with someone who had the nickname "transmit only"; he was difficult, boring and unpleasant. He never listened. When we are speaking we are in transmit mode. The goal is to be understood, however not to jam in as many ideas as possible.

Consider what words you choose, they will colour the depth of understanding. Use descriptive words... strong words... vivid words. Be enthusiastic and passionate, even if you are British! Seek a response. Use words that are visual (an *azure* blue sky), auditory (the *seagulls squawk*) and kinaesthetic (*running on the hot sand).*

Ask engaging questions, open-ended questions or rhetorical questions. Allow your audience to give back to you. When receiving, take a deep breath and...listen! Be spontaneous. Accept it as your role to a receiver. Don't fight it. Develop and hone you this speaking skill. People want to know they have been truly heard. It touches on their desire to be significant. Active listening involves acknowledging what's just been said to you; then playing it back in different words. Summarise what you have just heard. Do this and your audiences will embrace you. Speaking is an art with two winners – you and the audience.

Use props - both visible and invisible. I am known for using retro laser pointers. In fact, I give one to each delegate and use them in simple activities which help to anchor the talk key points.

What prop could you use and personalize?

If using props, keep them hidden until required. Ensure your prop can be seen from all parts of the room. Speak to the audience, not the prop (unless it is a puppet). The prop must be relevant to the message; if not don't use it. Take **Jill Bolte Taylor's** Ted Talk **http://www.ted.com/talks/jill_bolte_taylor_s_powerful_stroke_of_insight.html** when she uses a human brain during her amazing talk about the massive stroke that she had and the insights into life that she gained from it. The prop was effective because it gave the audience a highly visual, very memorable sense of the basic structure of the brain, which was important for the rest of the talk. You can download more prop tips from the Free Zone on my website.

Check out NSA speaker, **Tim Gard**. http://www.timgard.com/store/props.html Tim is inspirational in his use of props and even sells them on his personal shop. (See his link above).

Involve the audience in a variety of ways. Perhaps, task individual delegates to help or demonstrate aspects of your presentation. Have your audience participate by writing down a few words (recall the power of three?) or phrase. Ask them to fill in the blanks in a workbook or to say a short phrase to the person they are sitting beside. Games, puzzles and competitions can be fun if short and relevant; as can demonstrations and role play as they help to make your message stick.

If using music, make sure you have the rights to do so and rehearse the sound for peace of mind. When including a video clip prepare the text to voice-over the feature you want the video to highlight; unless the impact is so powerful that it stands alone.

Question-time can be tricky. If you entertain questions, make sure you answer them before you deliver your call-to-action. Your voice ought to be the last one the audience hears. It's important to let them know that you haven't finished your talk. e.g. "I have some concluding remarks, ladies and gentlemen, however now would be a good time to deal with your questions." Personally, I prefer to take questions during the talk. You just have to be mindful not to allow these to interrupt the flow or divert you away from your key material. It is your DNA that marks out your work, so you must control the Q&A.

Not all cultures will ask questions. The Finns for example would think it rude to ask a speaker a question. In their eyes, the presenter is the expert and therefore it would be rude to ask a question. They believe it would insult the speaker by implying that he/she had omitted vital information.

Finish with a crystal clear compelling call to action. Signal it is the end by stating *"... ladies and gentlemen, to close..."* You now have 30 seconds to state your call-to-action. What is it you want them to do? Any longer than half a minute and your audience will have moved their thoughts on to, the break, the next speaker or be fidgeting with their bags and brief cases, ready to leave.

In short, have a fantastic open... a powerful close...and be prepared to massage the body of your talk because one thing is guaranteed, at some point you will be asked to either extend it... or cut it by 20 minutes! Such is the lot of a speaker. That's when you need to be able to insert your fingerprints and plant footprints; the stories that must be told, the ones that only you can tell, the ones that audiences are waiting to hear.

Constantly practice to improve your speech. Review it regularly. Critique with people you respect and admire e.g. your mastermind group. Keep learning. Attend PSA conferences and regional meetings as part of your speaker development. Keep pruning. Let's face it; most speakers use far too many words. Keep injecting your DNA; the fundamental and distinctive characteristics and content that only you have the authority to use.

You can download a summary of this chapter at **http://www. eilidhmilnes.com/BookResources**

EILIDH MILNES *FPSA*

Eilidh - that's "Ay-lee" - is a teacher turned motivational speaker, columnist and award winning author. She is a member of the IFFPS (International Federation of Professional Speakers) a director the PSA UKI (Professional Speaking Association UK and Ireland) and National President 2014.

Drawing on more two decades of working as a qualified teacher, programme presenter and facilitator, Eilidh is now an internationally acclaimed keynote speaker. She works in both the public and private sectors well deserving her reputation as 'Captain Positive'. Her dynamic and impactful delivery has generated outstanding testimonials from her extensive client list. She delivers common sense solutions for everyday problems to help companies be more resilient. Her clients include PWC, BAE Systems, Morgan Stanley, Barclays and Hochtief.

Eilidh helps her clients see their way through domestic and work related issues. One of her corporate clients reported the following results after her workshops - a 2.3% reduction in sickness and a 2.71% reduction in attrition.

Tackling challenging issues such as the resolution of conflict, Eilidh's areas of specialist expertise includes professional development from presentation skills to time management and cross-cultural awareness. With a family of her own, Eilidh recognises the often conflicting priorities faced by those working in pressured and frequently stressful environments.

EMAIL: *e@eilidhmilnes.com*
PHONE: *+44 7876 786 784*
WEBSITES: *www.eilidhmilnes.com/ and www.thediversitydashboard.com/*
TWITTER: *@eilidhmilnes*
LINKEDIN: *www.uk.linkedin.com/in/theconfidencecoach*
FACEBOOK: *www.facebook.com/EilidhMilnesTheConfidenceCoach*
YOUTUBE: *www.youtube.com/user/ConfidenceTheCoach*

CHAPTER SEVEN

Managing Your State On and Off-Stage

FELIX A. SCHWEIKERT *FPSA*

"Honey, are you in the mood?" (for speaking)

So there you are. Behind the stage. Alone. You have done your preparation in advance: you have informed yourself about the audience, you have rehearsed your speech many times and you know your first three minutes of your speech like the back of your hand. All is well, if there were not those sweaty hands, those shaking knees and that hyperventilation. Even though you are thoroughly prepared you still have that feeling in you, that is more than just anxiety. It is fear. The fear that brings all those questions up, like "Will I find the right words?", "Will I remember the name of the CEO?", and "Will I be able to get my message across?"

Many speakers, especially the ones that are new to the business, face the situation of giving a speech badly prepared. Some of them do not prepare at all, they just give their speech. Then there are others who do prepare. They start out with researching the audience they are about to speak to, then they examine the venue and the stage they are going to be standing on, and lastly they plan their opening by learning it by heart so even if they become nervous, they are able to give the first one or two minutes without thinking. Some speakers even think thoroughly through all kind of distractions, hecklers and catastrophes that could occur during their speech and how they would react to them.

To cope with your nervousness and to become less and less nervous, you need to understand that preparation is your friend. Whatever preparation you do, it is better to prepare than not to prepare. And of course the more you prepare, the better you will be prepared and the less likely it will be that something unexpected happens. Do everything that is necessary and do almost everything that is possible to ensure your speaking success and minimise the possibility of failure.

Stage-state

What only very few speakers out there in the business work with, is the preparation of the state they are in, when they enter the stage; their stage-state. The stage-state is a combination of your beliefs and thoughts as well as your emotions and feelings when you enter the stage[1]. All these combined result in your stage-presence. The stage-presence is your "speaker-aura" which you emit on stage. This stage-presence is crucial, because for most of your audience this is the first impression they have of you when you enter the stage. It determines whether you succeed in winning the audience over in the first seconds or whether you are the one who will be dying on stage.

Many speakers are aware that there is a stage-state. The problem they have is that they do not know how to consciously alter that state to their benefit. But there is help. Today we know that there are various methods to change the state you are in when entering the stage, various methods to change your

---

[1] *It has to be stated, that the difference between emotions and feelings is broad and many academics disagree about their definitions. For the purpose of this chapter, the author uses the terms synonymously.*

beliefs, your thoughts and your emotions and feelings. All in all there exist possibilities to manage your emotional or mental state before you get onto the stage.

So let us examine the three elements that make up your stage-state:

1. **Beliefs**
2. **Thoughts**
3. **Emotions and Feelings**

Affirmations (Beliefs)

Your beliefs are very important, as they directly affect your thoughts, and these directly affect your emotions and feelings. Ask yourself the following questions: What are your beliefs concerning public speaking? What do you consider "true" or "false" when it comes to speaking from the platform? Do you believe in your success or your failure as speaker?

Your belief, or your belief system, is a combination of beliefs regarding your speaking. It is a result of your experiences but also of the experiences of your peers, and it affects your thoughts.

The great Zig Ziglar, who was author of many bestselling books and one of the highest paid speakers in the world, said that fear is an acronym for false evidence appearing real. Many times we take "false evidence" and adjust our reality accordingly. For example we have heard that "all speakers get sweaty hands before they enter the stage", so you get sweaty hands. Funnily enough though, some speakers do not get sweaty hands when they enter the stage. Do they live in a different universe? Don't they take their job seriously enough to not get sweaty hands? Or could it be that your belief about the sweaty hands is not true?

Write a list of every belief that you think affects your speaking. Check this list to see if the beliefs you have hinder your speaking career or if they support it. As long as they support you and your speaking business, everything is fine and there is no need to worry. But if there are some beliefs or assumptions that do not help you to be a great speaker, then it is time to re-think that "truth".

Some speakers use short prayers before they enter the stage to focus on their strength and the strength and power behind them. The great international speaker Dottie Walters asked God for help by praying the words of St. Francis of Assissi: "Lord, let me be a channel of Your love."

You can also use so-called "affirmations" to support your beliefs to change from negative to positive. Affirmations are carefully formatted statements which you repeat to yourself and also write them down and carry them with you in case you want to read through them.

Tell yourself "I love each member of my audience, I know they are all supportive, they all want me to succeed" over and over again when you enter the stage. Also think of the reasons why the audience already does love you and why they will love you even more after you have given your speech.

For an affirmation to be effective, it needs to be the present tense, expressed positively and specific only for you. Here are some examples of good affirmations:

- *I feel great.*
- *I am in a positive mood.*
- *(I know) I will succeed.*
- *I am a great and professional speaker.*
- *I speak clearly and my audience listens to me.*

When you say these affirmations to you over and over again you will notice that the words will sink in and you will actually believe the words you say yourself, and not only your beliefs will change but also the thoughts, emotions and feelings deriving from them.

Change focus (Thoughts)

Your thoughts directly affect your emotions and feelings and are very important for your stage-state. Ask yourself the following questions: What are your thoughts when you enter the stage today? Are these thoughts helpful? In what way do these thoughts support or hinder your speech and/or you as a speaker?

It was proven by researchers and coaches, especially in sports, that the human brain is consciously only able to concentrate on one single thought or task at a given moment. And most speakers concentrate only on their speech the moment they walk up stage. So far so good. This has to be so, especially if you have not memorised the first sentence or the first minute of your speech (or even your entire speech). So how would it be if you were concentrating on something else in that moment, because you did memorise your first minute?

Some speakers think that they will fail, that they are badly prepared and that the audience hates them. I am not saying that 100% of them fail in the end or that they are bad speakers, but they do have a harder time being great. So why don't you do it differently?

You cannot afford to let negativity in your head manifest itself. You simply should not let any negativity into your mind the moment you enter the stage. So focus on something positive and uplifting before you enter the stage.

It may also be beneficial if you change the focus of your thinking. When speakers enter the stage, many of them think of things like their failure or even failures in the past, bad moments or hecklers in the audience. This thinking is mostly accompanied by pictures and sounds of these moments and of course affects their emotions and feelings.

Changing your focus means you use pictures of very positive moments in your speaking career or other beautiful life-moments and recall them in your mind. You think of the pictures associated with these moments: Where were you exactly? Who was there with you? What did the surrounding look like? What colours did you see? Then you think of the sounds or even smell or tastes in that moment: What sounds did you hear? Was there music in the air? Did you taste something specific in that moment? Was there a distinct smell?

If you manage to visualise the moment as clearly as possible, you may be able to recall that particular moment in front of your inner eye, and by doing so you will notice the joyful emotions and feelings of that moment to reappear in you as well.

You can also support the process of visualisation by using a short break before you start visualising. That short break needs only to be a few seconds and can be as short as a long deep breath.

Act as if (Emotions and feelings)

One method to change your emotions and feelings is by choosing the way you act. First and foremost you have to realise that not only do your emotions and feelings affect the way you behave, but also the way you behave affects your emotions and feelings. For example, when you recall a moment in your life that was very joyful and you were feeling very happy, you may notice that your muscles relax, your shoulders fall down softly and that your jaw relaxes as well. There is a connection of certain emotions and feelings with certain reactions of your body towards those emotions and feelings.

It can be said that you need to act or behave in a certain way in order to that feeling to come through to you. You cannot stand still, have your shoulders hanging down, your head bent forward, looking to the ground and feel happy. You need to stand "in a happy way". This could be upright, your head held up high, with your eyes looking forward or up and your arms raised high in the air. This time you will manage to feel happy because your body matches your emotions.

You can use this now by acting confidently if you need confidence. You will notice that over time the emotions and feelings will come just from behaving confidently.

If you have no idea how to act confidently, think of a person that has the confidence you need in that moment. How would that person behave in that moment? You could even think of someone no longer living or a fictional character that has the resources (e.g. confidence) you need in that particular moment. How would that person have reacted? What would that character do? ("How would Superman handle this?")

Music (Emotions and feelings)

Music has been known for centuries to affect the emotions and feelings of the people listening to it. So think about incorporating music into your preparation shortly before your appearance on stage.

The style of music depends on your personal preferences and should be uplifting and motivational. Even if you love a certain piece of music but it brings up mixed feelings for example because you always think of your former love affair, you should not use this in your preparation.

Here is a list of some pieces of music the author or other international successful speakers use "to get them in the right mood":

- *"Holding out for a Hero" by Bonnie Tyler*
- *"We are the Champions" by Queen*
- *Theme from "Pirates of the Caribbean"*
- *Theme from "Rocky" (including opening fanfare)*
- *Other movie themes e.g. from John Williams (Star Wars, Superman, Indiana Jones, ...)*

Summary

By implementing the above techniques you will be able to get yourself in the right mood for speaking by improving your stage-state and your stage presence. This will lead to greater confidence and you will be able to speak better, amaze your audience and get more speaking engagements.

FELIX A. SCHWEIKERT *FPSA*

Felix assists others in their aim to search and find more success in their lives. His motto for his audience is: *"Supreme success through passion, patience and persistence."*

He holds two degrees in Business with an expertise in marketing, consulting and business communication. After having finished his training as a banker and having graduated in Ludwigshafen/Germany and Leeds/United Kingdom he founded his own training company at the age of 26.

Felix is one of the highest awarded speakers in Europe. He is member of the TOP 100 of Trainers Excellence and was awarded "Premium-Quality-Expert" five years in a row. He is the only German to be awarded the Platinum Seal of Trainer-Ranking.com where over 500 customers voted him 9.4 out of 10 in all 10 categories. In April 2013 he was voted Speaker of the Year and was made the first Fellow of the Professional Speakers Association outside the United Kingdom.

With German as his mother tongue as well as fluent English, Felix trains and speaks internationally in both languages. His clients achieve great results after his trainings and they come from a wide range of industries: banks and insurances, hotels, but also plant engineering. The size ranges from the top 10 in Germany to small and medium sized companies.

EMAIL: *felix@felix-schweikert.com*

TELEPHONE: *+49 6205 20 48 663*

FAX: *+49 6205 25 59 01*

WEBSITE: *www.felix-schweikert.com*

CHAPTER EIGHT

Presenting your Keynote with Confidence

KATE ATKIN *FPSA*

What is Confidence?

Confidence is one of those odd phenomena where you often don't realise you have it, until suddenly it is gone and you feel the loss of it! It's often this lack of confidence that people notice, so the issue is: can you generate more confidence when you need it and what has it got to do with keynote speaking?

The word confidence comes from the Latin verb confidere, meaning to have full trust or reliance. Personally, I describe confidence as a "healthy dollop of self-belief, with a sprinkling of humility". The element of humility is important here, without it, as a speaker, we risk falling into the trap of arrogance. A trap which leads us to focus on our own needs, rather than those of our audience, and we start to think that having self-confidence is all about ourselves, and our performance. It isn't! At least that's my view. Your audience are attentive for a reason... they wish to learn something, do something differently or feel inspired, as speakers we need the confidence to deliver this.

Of course, in the absence of confidence, many public speakers wouldn't be able get up and deliver a keynote speech, so there has to be a certain baseline level of confidence that we already possess. However, there are times when as a speaker we feel a confidence wobble. It may be triggered by performing for a new client, a larger audience than we are used to, new material, or perhaps something in our personal lives is having an effect. Whatever it is that's causing the confidence wobble it isn't something you can show during your keynote because your audience need to believe what you are saying; they need to have confidence in both you and your message. So I'm going to take this opportunity to provide you with some tips, tricks and techniques you can use to give your confidence a boost when you need to. Try them out and then decide which ones work for you.

Fake it till you make it

You may have heard this phrase, and for some people it really works. So if this one's for you, it means that you aim to act the part, displaying behaviours that outwardly suggest confidence, despite your churning insides. This means putting on a smile, straightening your posture, relaxing your shoulders, speaking slowly and clearly and giving your keynote your best shot.

Use the feedback you get to work out which were the good bits of acting, focus on those and tweak anything that needs to be changed before you do it again. Practice as an actor would and somewhere along the line you will find that your underlying confidence actually grows to match your persona, often without you being consciously aware.

Of course, the problem with this approach is that you are not necessarily being genuine to yourself up on stage, and audiences may pick up on this. This is especially the case if your keynote includes a lot of autobiographical stories, which need to be told 'from the heart' rather than acted, to gain empathy and engagement from the audience. In these cases being brave enough to open up and show a lack of confidence might be beneficial, both to you and your audience. By being your true self you are giving your audience permission to have doubts too, showing you are also human and making your keynote real and accessible.

Creating Confidence before your Keynote

You might wish to build up your confidence before you deliver your keynote rather than rely on the 'fake it' strategy. There are several ways to do this, and I'll outline some of them here:

1. Do your five-in-a-day

Research in positive psychology has shown that doing five happiness enhancing actions in a single day boosts your happiness more than five actions spread out over a week. Confidence is closely correlated to happiness, after all it is difficult to feel confident when you are unhappy, so it is not unreasonable to assume that the five-in-a-day rule applies to confidence as well.

What could your 'five-in-a-day' confidence boosting actions be? This will depend on your own personal circumstances but it may include doing something that you find challenging, such as speaking to a complete stranger (how about holding a conversation with a Big Issue seller), making that sales call either by phone or in person, going to a networking event and speaking to five people you haven't met before, taking improv lessons or metaphorically putting yourself on a milk crate on Speakers Corner. They don't have to be big actions, however, just something you wouldn't normally do in a day... it could be something simple like picking up some litter, holding the door open for someone, giving someone a compliment or thanking a shop assistant.

All of these types of actions give us a little 'phew, I did it moment' after the event, a little glow of achievement and self-confidence. It is the cumulative effect of these moments that builds confidence. So maybe give yourself some 'phew' moments in the days and hours leading up to that important keynote. I'm not necessarily suggesting looking out for lots of Big Issue sellers on the way to the venue, but find actions that work for you, in your particular circumstances.

2. Build your Confidence Wall

Reflecting back on past achievements also helps to create a sense of well-being and a "can-do" attitude. Often we forget or downplay our past successes as they can seem insignificant; learning to drive may seem trivial now, but at the time passing your driving test might have been a major boost to your self-confidence. Remembering and reflecting on significant past achievements can provide us with a boost to our self-esteem in the present.

I call the process of doing this building your Confidence Wall, but there are other variations. To build your Confidence Wall, take a piece of paper and draw a brick wall, with the bricks large enough to write in. Inside each brick write a few words to remind you of a specific moment in time that, when you think of it, makes you feel good. For example, don't write "my family", but do write "the birth of my son" or "teaching my daughter to read". Other examples could be taking time out last week to spend with a friend, giving a talk at your old school, baking a cake for Fred or competing in the golf tournament.

Take your time over this, and once you have filled out as many bricks as you can, take a few minutes to reflect on the moments you have recorded on your wall. Where were you? Who were you with? What was being said? How did you feel? Then make your wall accessible so it is there to look at, review and give you a boost when you need it. Some people put it on their study wall, some make an electronic version and keep it on their smartphone, others miniaturise it and keep it in their wallet or purse, or you could make a picture version, whatever works for you.

Take out your confidence wall and reflect on it before that critical speaking engagement, it will help you to remember the things you have achieved, the good moments, and help push those negative thoughts away.

3. Watch your Thinking

So it's a big keynote presentation coming up... how are you feeling? Stop! Check your thinking. As Felix said in chapter 7, your thoughts determine what happens on stage. What is running through your mind? Our thoughts encourage our brains to secrete certain hormones; happy thoughts make happy hormones such as endorphins, oxytocin and dopamine, but negative thoughts make stress hormones, such as cortisol. So we have a positive feedback loop in our brain: Confident thoughts result in changes in brain chemistry that sustain and build happiness and confidence. On the other hand, a negative cycle can so easily be set up, whereby we get trapped in a loop of negative thoughts causing stress and anxiety changes in brain chemistry that just lead to yet more negative thoughts. This is the root cause of mental health conditions such as depression and anxiety disorders, but hopefully we are not talking about that here, just making sure that those common or garden 'butterflies' don't grow to the point where they damage your speaking effectiveness.

So as you think about your forthcoming speech, what is it you are thinking? "I can do it, I know my stuff, I am good at what I do"? or "Why did I say yes to this one? Will I be good enough?" The important thing here is to remind yourself that it is not all about you. Take a moment to think about your audience as well. Why will they be there? What are they expecting? What do you want to leave them with? How would you like them to feel? Focussing your thoughts on the client and the audience may take some of the pressure off you and allow your mind to open up, rather than close down and become locked into that negative, self-centred thought cycle. It can encourage you to think of the event as a situation where you and the audience are working together to achieve a desired goal, rather than as a show in which you, the performer, have to wow and impress the audience with your amazing personality. (Unless of course you are doing stand-up comedy, but most business keynotes don't call for that.)

4. Stand Tall

While you are working on noticing your thinking, also take a moment to notice your posture. When you think negatively what happens? Your shoulders start to slump, a frown forms on your face and you hug yourself more readily. When we think positive, confident thoughts, the opposite happens... your shoulders straighten, you smile more readily and you stand taller with your arms more relaxed. No great surprise there, but what I find so fascinating is that the relationship works in the other direction as well. Your posture can actually direct your thinking because your brain and body are so closely linked that the brain takes cues from what is happening in your body. Of course we know this is true in the extreme case of trauma, where damage to our body produces pain sensations which can stop any other thoughts dead in their tracks. But it also works with posture, albeit in a much more subtle manner.

So when we stand with an erect confident posture, we actually find it harder to think negatively and easier to think positive thoughts. Go on, try it out now. Think of a moment when things didn't go so well. Focus on it for a moment; who were you with, what was being said, how were you feeling? Now try and remember your posture. Next, think of a time when things went really well. Who were you with, what was being said, how were you feeling? Now notice your posture. Finally, and most usefully, take a moment to adopt a really positive posture, straighten your back, relax your shoulders and your arms and put a smile on your face (a Duchenne smile involving the eye muscles, not a fake grin). While holding that posture, think of the negative situation you had in mind a moment ago. Notice I said, while holding that posture... I suggest that you'll find it hard to really access those negative thoughts without your posture slumping in response, so keep that back straight, shoulders square and smile!

In summary, to be able to present your next keynote with confidence, focus on your posture. Plan your different body positions during certain parts of your talk, make sure you know how you want to appear and at the very start, begin with a really confident stance.

5. Breathe

Breathing happens naturally, thankfully, but when we feel stressed, our breathing becomes shallow and fast. We tend then to breathe from the upper part of the chest. The top parts of our lungs have less room to expand, so our lungs transfer less oxygen into the bloodstream. This means less oxygen is reaching your brain, so we think less clearly and also your heart has to beat faster to pump the limited oxygen supply around your body. Recognise the symptoms?

So breathe deeply, instead! Taking just three deep breaths before you go up on stage can help to calm the nerves, settle your heart rate and will give you enough air in your lungs to make a powerful opening with your voice.

6. Visualise

Linked to technique number 3, Watch your Thinking, Visualisation is a specific direction of your thoughts into the future. If you find tip 3 useful this one is also likely to work well for you. When thinking about your forthcoming keynote stop worrying about whether you will get up onto the stage without tripping up, whether the microphone will work or whether your slide presentation will freeze when you are mid sentence. Instead see your keynote going well. In your mind's eye imagine you arrive in plenty of time, speak to the sound engineers and have all the technology tested and working well before you go onto the stage. Use your imagination to walk up onto the stage, deliver your keynote and give the audience and client exactly what they need.

Running through your speech with a "what goes well" scenario rather than a "what could go wrong" scenario enables your brain to see just how you want to perform. It will then help you during your actual speech as you will not only have rehearsed aloud, but also in your mind, and the brain is amazingly powerful at providing what we focus on.

This doesn't mean there is no need to plan for what might go wrong. Going through those scenarios ensures you have back-ups in hand, such as putting your slides onto a data stick and into Dropbox or another Cloud form, just in case... However, if you hold the ideas of what could go wrong in your head the night before you are due to speak and in the minutes before you step onto the platform your brain will be seeking out the troublesome aspects, providing you with cortisol (remember the stress hormone?) and not filling you with confidence to give the best performance you are able to do.

So, to give your audience the best possible keynote, visualise every step going right. I do this just before I go to sleep the night before and again when I am at the venue.

7. One Big Thing

At a conference I attended recently I had the opportunity to ask a couple of the speakers how they dealt with their fears. One of them replied that they focussed on having overcome one big thing in their life, and after that, they measured every other challenge by that milestone.

So if you have achieved one very large, significant thing in your eyes, it doesn't have to be significant in anyone else's, this might be the strategy for you. Relive the moment, what you did, how you felt at the time and how you felt having overcome it.

Now compare that with your current situation. Can you bring any of the lessons into the present?

8. Coping with Fear

If you use all the above tips you might well feel that you will have your confidence sorted. So why have I put a section about coping with fear into this chapter on delivering your keynote with confidence? Using the tips, tricks and techniques above will indeed help you to present a truly authentic, confident keynote; however, they don't guarantee you will be fear-free.

Having an element of fear, or nerves as I prefer to call them, provides an edge of adrenaline. It is this adrenaline which stops us from becoming blasé about our work. Sometimes though, the nerves can get a little too much. The first thing to do is to realise that everyone has them. If you feel nervous, recognise you are in good company; Dame Judy Dench has spoken out about her own nerves when giving live performances, despite years of experience and success, and as speakers we are also giving live performances.

To cope with fear, and deal with your nerves, acknowledge them and don't berate yourself for feeling the way you do. Once acknowledged, decide what you want to do with your fear... Do you want to use visualisation to see your nerves as butterflies flying in formation, or put them into a metaphorical box to look at later, or widen your focus, as widening your peripheral vision helps prevent you from becoming fixated on the fear itself?

Personally I like the strategy of creating a "worry box" in which you put down your worries explicitly on paper. Writing down your fears objectifies and externalises them and helps you to look at them more rationally. Instead of throwing away the paper, pop it somewhere safe, with a deadline date - the time by which the fear will either have been realised or passed, usually the date of your speech. Once in a while, say each month, go through your worries and re-read those whose deadline date has passed. I find it puts them into perspective as they so rarely come to pass.

So there you have it, eight tips, tricks and techniques to help you present your next keynote with confidence. Combined with the other tips in this book you'll be well on your way to "speaking more and speaking better".

KATE ATKIN *FPSA*

If you are looking for a speaker to boost the confidence of your staff, increase the productivity of teams, or the effectiveness of that perennial nutshell "communication" then give Kate Atkin a call. Kate specialises in inspiring courageous conversations, strengthening inner resilience and driving optimal performance. With over fifteen years' experience of working with a wide variety of organisations, teams and individuals Kate has a proven track record and uses her own life and work experiences to help others.

Since starting her own business in 2000, over 90% of Kate's work has come through personal recommendation. She has spoken to audiences in Las Vegas, Malta, Jersey, Barcelona, Mongolia and of course in the UK. Kate has been recognised as the Most Outstanding Trainer and Most Outstanding Mentor in JCI UK, has been nominated for Cambridgeshire Businesswoman of the Year and is a World Debating Champion. She also has an academic interest in the emerging discipline of positive psychology and is currently reading for a Masters degree.

Kate is a fellow of the Professional Speaking Association and a member of the Chartered Institute for Personnel and Development and the Association for Coaching. She is also an associate of the Chartered Institute of Bankers and a Senator of Junior Chamber International.

EMAIL: **kate@kateatkin.com**

TELEPHONE: **+44 (0) 7779 646 976**

WEBSITE: **www.kateatkin.com**

TWITTER: **@kateatkin**

LINKEDIN: **www.linkedin.com/in/kateatkin**

FACEBOOK: **www.facebook.com/theconfidentmanager**

CHAPTER NINE

The Art of Storytelling

DAVID HYNER *FPSA*

Once upon a time...

Don't worry, we will not go there !

There was once a chef who wanted so badly to be a professional speaker that he believed that he would do almost anything to;

- *receive the acclaim of an audience*
- *live the jet set life of an international professional speaker*
- *and earn the higher fees that top speakers earn*

He created a talk that went down very well, although if he were honest, he would say that it had a few bits of "other people's material" within it. Blissfully ignorant of the seriousness of his deeds, he thought that in some way the owners of that content would thank him for exposing others to their work, even though he rarely credited them in his talks. He thought he was doing "okay".

Then one day a client asked about the speaker's background, and when he had shared a little of his background and research to the client, a request was made for him to talk about his own research and tell of his own experiences and stories.

As the speaker created this talk for the clients conference he was amazed at just how many experiences he had to draw upon that would add genuine value to an audience, and soon was creating his own content that was (years later) to become the very reason he got booked to speak to between 10,000 – 50,000 people a year all over the UK, and at times, internationally.

The conference soon came around and when presenting, he noticed how much more certainty he had when delivering. He didn't have to try. He was able to live his experiences out in front of the audience in a way that was true to him, and they lapped it up.

He noticed the difference after the talk as well, for in addition to the polite applause and acclaim he was now used to getting, he had delegates saying things like "I am going to use this to..." and "this is going to make a difference to...."

As weeks and months passed he would then receive emails and calls saying "I used that technique and I have achieved ...." Etc

Thirteen years later after discovering that purpose is more important than "the purse", he

- *Receives emails and letters from delegates who have made a (sometimes HUGE) difference to their own, or others' lives by using his research content.*

- *Noticed that train stations, airport departure lounges and eating room service meals in a hotel bedroom is hardly "jet set"*

- *And that he can earn just as much if not more by working smarter, and by doing so, spend more time at home with those he loves the most in the world.*

His speaking business grew as a direct result of creating and telling his own stories, and those from his research.

Now whilst the above details my own journey to date as a speaker, it covers my first top tip for telling a great story.

Tip 1

If possible and appropriate, use your own stories and experiences, or those you have directly researched.

You may be a speaker that delivers technical information, statistics or detail driven content where there is no place for storytelling..... think again.

If a financial director can abseil onto a stage and deliver a set of annual accounts in a "mission impossible" themed story, there is hope for any of us, eh? And yes.... That actually happened, and yes, people still talk about that talk years later.

A great story captures our imagination, hearts and minds and takes us with the speaker as they subtly weave their message into the story whilst holding our attention for long periods of time.

This happens because if a good story is being told it obliges the recipient to create images in their mind, emotions that feel very real to us, and to listen to, process, and consider what is being said by the speaker.

This way a great story can hook even the most sceptical of audience members .... if delivered with integrity.

Tip 2

Be authentic and tell the story as if you were living it

By this I mean use your voice, facial expression, gesture, body language to deliver the story. Use language and tonality to tell the audience what you saw and heard, "show them" how it made you feel, describe smells, tastes or sensations it evoked within you.

Live the story on stage as if you were in the moment. There are certain limits to this where maybe a speaker has such an emotional story that it reduces the audience and themselves to tears every time they deliver. Now at times it cannot be helped, but the stage is not a place for therapy (for the speaker). The power must come from the story and not from the speakers need for emotional release.

I have seen speakers with a "purpose" who have had no speaking training yet command a room who hang on their every word due to the conviction in their voice, for their fear is dwarfed by their desire for their message to be heard.

The more passionate you are about the story or message, the easier it is to be authentic.

For example, if I were to talk about how important it is to read small print in a contract this sounds a pretty dull subject (to many people... not all).

I could say *"I once was nearly put out of business when there was a contractual blunder and some adverts were printed incorrectly"*, or..... I could say;

"All they had to do was reprint my advert the same as last years. Because of this, no proof of design was needing a signature, they said. Weeks later I received the directory and with childish anticipation thumbed the pages to find my advert. As I reached

the page my eyes scanned the text and images until they came to rest upon my advert. My heart sank. I felt as if life force itself was draining from me. A numbness crept over me as I dropped the directory on the floor, but within seconds my blood began to boil with rage as my mind turned to the reality of the situation.

They had printed my advert ... but with my main competitor's phone number on instead of my own!"

If the second one was being presented with feeling and emotion, showing you with expression and gesture the full shock of the situation, I would wager that you would probably have wanted to have seen the second version despite it being much longer.

More (appropriate) detail gives more credibility to the speaker and the content, and hooks the receiver into the message.

Doing this you can work with teenagers, corporate teams or CEO groups and still engage most if not all of the room with your message.

To start with though, we should also consider where we get stories from.

Here are a few ideas;

1. *Use your own adventures, experiences, relationships, disasters and triumphs, and if you do not have any.... Go out and get some. Climb a mountain, run a business, do charity work, write a book, do some research, wrestle a crocodile. Okay, maybe not the crocodile, but you get the point.*

2. *Research the subject until you are an authority on it.*

3. *Interview top achievers in that field of endeavour.*

4. *Do a poll or survey to obtain data that shocks or surprises.*

5. *Work colleagues, friends, families, online networks will all have their own stories that you could adapt if needs be, with their permission.*

It is Important to stress that if you use another person's content or story, it is professional, polite, and legally obliging to obtain their permission to use it, and courteous to refer to them as the original source in your delivery.

See how easy it is to do this by writing down an example of a story from your own experiences in life:

1. *An example of great leadership from a former boss*

2. *One thing NEVER to do when you are a leader based on an experience you had or witnessed with a leader.*

3. *An example of amazing or less than perfect customer service...*

4. *Listening skills (good or bad)*

Easy isn't it?

Tip 3

Know "why" you are telling the story

If you are using a story to pad, or fill time then please do not use a story. It will reek of insincerity when you present it. Instead ask yourself if the message would be enhanced or remembered better if delivered within a great story.

Are you telling the story to feel better about yourself? If so then do not tell the story.

Only tell stories that are going to help the audience understand how THEY can think and behave differently or become more effective themselves after applying something they have learnt from hearing this story.

The only exception to this are those speakers that are hired to tell their life story or story of success alone with little need for take-away value, or return on the client's investment on the speaker.

If you are a more extrovert speaker, or if being expressive comes easy to you, then I would urge you to consider using stories. If you are a more reserved personality I would urge you to rehearse your delivery to ensure that you are comfortable being expressive and open on stage.

It suits some more than others, but if we can "get out of our own way" when delivering the story, our message comes to life in a way that little else can achieve.

It is always a good idea to test your stories on smaller groups and in non-fee paying events before risking a new part of a talk or story at a fee paying event.

Tip 4

Involve your audience in the story

I am known for telling a few stories in my presentations and one of these is a story about overcoming adversity as experienced by a top achiever I interviewed. This person had overcome the most incredible adversity and setbacks to achieve at the highest level in sport and other areas of life.

The story was already powerful and was a key milestone in my delivery when one day I presented the talk to a group of fourteen year old students in a high school. The group were talented and clever young adults, yet they lacked confidence, and many of them had been identified as having "situations" either within or outside of school that were holding them back.

The story is an "excuse buster!"... so I went for it.

I was five minutes from closing my talk when I paused, looked into their eyes and asked them to think of the one excuse that they were using to stop them doing the things in life that they wanted to do. I asked them;

"I want you to come with me as I tell you this true story as if this were happening to you, and at every turn please ask yourself what you would have done in this person's situation. Furthermore at the end of the story I would ask you to consider how valid your excuses are?"

I went on to deliver the story and when finished I was overwhelmed with the response from the audience.

The next day I presented to three hundred adults at a trade association conference and did exactly the same thing, with the same response.

The next week the same happened in a leadership group.

By involving the audience and inviting them into your story in some way that makes it personal to them, they engage with the speaker and their message like never before. It becomes about "them" rather than about the speaker (as it should be).

Tip 5

Stories are everywhere

Just because you have a story does not mean you have to use it, but there are opportunities to embed your information in the hearts and minds of your delegates by using a knockout story in the right place and at the right time.

I often use a story at the start or end of a talk, or if the audience's attention is drifting a little (to grab them back).

The way we use stories can be varied and here are a few examples of how you can use a story to get your message across;

- *Rather than explain a sales technique tell a story about how a sales professional used the technique.*

- *If your audience is facing a call to action or need to overcome challenge, rather than say "we need to do this..." you can use an empowering true story of somebody who has overcome incredible odds and challenge to achieve explaining how they did it, and how we can do the same.*

- *If delivering a leadership technique, say how a business leader turned their business around by using this information.*

- *Rather than talk about customer service best practise, tell a story of an awesome customer experience you received, and how your audience could do the same for their clients.*

- *..... Need we go on?*

Sometimes I use a story of a teenager who went from C/D borderline in his science grades to gaining a GCSE (English high school exam level) A* with 100% grade within four months. All he had done was apply himself to thinking and behaving differently to how he had previously done using the techniques I had given him.

What great messages do you have that would have a greater impact if delivered as a story rather than a case study?

Have fun !

DAVID HYNER *FPSA*

David grew and sold a catering and event management business before turning his hobby of researching top achievers into his passion for personal effectiveness. Many years later he is one of few people in the world who have interviewed many top achievers on the subject of goal setting and achievement.

His fun, challenging and inter-active style gives audiences the confidence and skills they need to achieve more, giving clients more time, resource and profit.

David speaks in the UK and internationally.

Co-author of two Amazon no. 1 books, formerly presented a BBC radio show on positive thinking, and is much in demand for corporate events, team days and education sector keynotes and workshops.

A passionate speaker who cares about your audience, and their purpose.

David says that "personal development is too full of fluff. I give it a kick!"

❝One of the best, if not THE best speaker I have ever seen❞
BARCLAYCARD

WEBSITE: ***www.davidhyner.com***

TWITTER: ***@davidhyner***

CHAPTER TEN

PowerPoint Surgery: How to create presentation slides that make your message stick

LEE JACKSON *FPSA*

3 types of speakers

There are 3 types of speakers in the world. The first love slides, they embrace them and they use them effectively to enhance their talks. They understand what makes a good slide and apply those rules for maximum impact.

The second don't use slides at all. They ignore them because they don't need them or they don't want to use them, and that's great. There are some excellent speakers in that category and I occasionally agree with them and do that myself. Not all talks need slides - eulogies are a classic example! Dr. Martin Luther King Jnr. didn't suffer from the lack of slides, neither did JFK or Obama.

However, I'm much more concerned about the third type of public speaker, a speaker who says they don't use or like slides but they use them anyway! This gets them into all sorts of trouble. An experienced speaker once told me, "I work very hard on my talks, Lee, but I just throw some slides together". I didn't know what to say. He just wasn't bothered. He doesn't throw his stories and message together as he's a great speaker, so why would he throw his slides together? It's bizarre.

A phrase that strikes fear into my heart is when a speaker stands and says; "I haven't had time to prepare so I'm just going to read from my slides". This is usually followed by the speaker turning their back on the audience to commence their public reading exercise. You may laugh but I have genuinely seen this.

Even worse, I've heard this: "I'm very nervous, so I'm just going to read from my slides, [they gave out a small nervous laugh] these aren't even my slides, and I haven't had time to look at them!" We thought he was joking - he wasn't. That's an hour of my life I'll never get back. Similarly a friend of mine who works for a speakers' bureau recalls how on her MA course one student copied the whole of their research paper onto slides and just read it out to the class with their back turned. Shocking stuff.

There is a better way.

> *If your words or images are not on point, making them dance in colour won't make them relevant...Power corrupts, PowerPoint corrupts absolutely.*
>
> **EDWARD TUFTE, YALE EMERITUS PROFESSOR**

Firstly, don't pass on the blame

The engrained business philosophy of 'slides are the presentation' is a major problem that needs addressing.

My philosophy is simple - if our slides are bad, don't blame the software, or our audience, it's our fault. If our football team loses, we don't blame FIFA (except for the lack of goal-line technology - don't get me started), we blame the manager, we blame the team. If our train is late, we blame the train operator, not George Stephenson! When I coach my business clients on slides they often say to me that their boss forces them to use 'the company slides', so not using the 'standard corporate slide pack' is seen as being rude or disrespectful to their boss. PowerPoint has waaaay too much power in the corporate world. It's not on the board, it's not a shareholder, we need to treat it as what it is - a piece of computer code that we can use for good, or for evil.

The software that we use, whether it's Microsoft PowerPoint, Apple Keynote (my programme of choice), Prezi, Slideshark, Haiku Deck or the various other open source programs out there, the issue remains the same.

All of these programs aren't inherently bad, they are neutral, they are just tools for us to use.

So how do we make slides better?

Here are a few tips. Simple advice that can change your slides forever, IF you have the guts to implement them!

You are a designer!

Whether you like it or not, as soon as you open your slide design programme you instantly become a designer. My designer mate Paul Kerfoot had a go at me a while back when I said to him "I'm not a designer, Paul, I just love making good slides". He made me realise that of course, we are all designers - it's not a choice we have once we use presentation software. The penny dropped.

Designer's Tip: Most designers, photographers and cameramen use 'the rule of thirds' aka the 'golden ratio', or the 'divine proportion'. Next time you see an interview on the news, look where the person is standing in the shot.

Simply put, they are probably filling one or two thirds of the screen, people rarely put their subjects in the middle of the screen anymore. Why? Because it looks better, it's more appealing and natural for us especially now we have widescreen. So when you are arranging your slides think in thirds. Fill one or two thirds of the screen, don't always centre everything. Try it and start to notice it. You'll begin to see it everywhere, in photos, paintings, food packaging, even nature. There are all sorts of calculations and ratios involved but basically think in thirds and your slides will become much more appealing to your audience.

Don't do the default!

When you open up PowerPoint or Keynote you usually get a default template option.

When you see that option STOP right there, go no further!

Do not take the default option, which is usually a main title followed by bullet-points. Instead, open a blank slide in the colour of your choice, add a picture if you are using them, and then if necessary a large text box.

You can often change the default option too in your software's preferences or options.

Change it so you don't fall into the default trap next time you are starting up PowerPoint.

It takes a lot of discipline to do this, but so do most things worth doing.

Get a blank white template here for free - **http://leejackson. org/powerpoint-surgery-stuff**

Think billboard, NOT document!

This is where the rot sets in; people simply try to do too many things with their slides. Fundamentally, slides are for the audience, not for us the speaker. Although I admit it's tempting, they should not be our crutch. Once we understand that they are for our audience, we design them in a bigger and bolder way. Feel free to make a word document to hand out after your talk if you like (although no-one ever reads those documents in my experience), but don't make your slides in that way. Build them for the bored bloke in row 33. Nancy Duarte helpfully compared slides to billboards in her book Slide:ology. Imagine you are passing your slides at 50mph on a major road. Could you read them as you drive past? If you can't they are too complicated and wordy. It's a simple but effective test for designers like us.

Design your slides and if appropriate write some handout notes.

But, just to be absolutely clear they are two very separate things!

If you're going to produce a presentation slide deck, then do just that - don't be tempted to make it into a hand-out with a slightly larger font.*

Bullets kill

Bullets don't just kill people, they kill presentations too. The default template may try to force you to use bullets, but you're a grown up now and as I mentioned - you can say no. Sometimes when I see speakers present a slide with bullet points you can almost feel the people in the room deflate, they may not groan out loud, but they are inside.

Sometimes people have an hour to speak using 30 slides with 10 bullet points on each slide, written in Comic Sans at font size

10. Not only do people get bored when they see this, they can read it too. People can read much faster than you can speak.

Therefore if you read your bullet points, they've read ahead of you already and you are speaking 'old information' even before a word leaves your mouth. As discussed previously, people can read or listen; they can't usually do both, even if they say they can. That's why slides should be bullet-free zones, no-one likes them, they are not effective, and to be honest they are just plain lazy, we can do better than that. So for our audience's sake - please please please don't use bullets.

On a train journey I was sitting next to someone doing a research paper and she was copying her bullet points from her slides directly into her word document. They fitted perfectly, because they belonged in the word document not on the presentation slide.

I've heard it said to limit the words on a slide to 33. I'd say 3-12! Any more than that then rephrase, condense or add another slide. There are creative alternatives to bullet points, but be careful you don't just design nicer ways to bore your audience. Be tough on bullet boredom and the causes of bullet boredom.

Use Images, but remember - This isn't the 90's

Home Alone, Wayne's World and *Titanic* were king in the 90's - along with clipart.

People couldn't get enough of quirky hand drawn stick figures with question marks above their heads. Then as the 90's progressed we moved into cheesy stock photos, and we were all introduced to that picture of the world with two anonymous business people's hands shaking in front of it. I still see that now.

Some people even used sounds on their slides, a "bing" to announce the change of slide, a "clunk" to wake up the audience when a new bullet point appears. We loved it. Those days have gone. We might like watching Titanic again once in a while (the boat sinks by the way, a friend of ours didn't realise that and she was gutted when it happened in the film) but we really need to drag our slides into this decade.

Here's how: ditch the clipart, sounds and cheesy stock pictures and go for big pictures that fill the screen.

Choose your pictures carefully, never choose the most popular photos on stock sites (see the techie section near the end of this book for more help) and make sure the image is big enough to fill the screen without getting grainy or pixelated. That makes a big difference. Remember your laptop screen is fairly small and a big screen will show up all the imperfections in the image, so buy or find decent size images but not too big so they get too unwieldy.

Use 'random internet' or 'Googled' images with caution, beware of copyright and quality. Most of us have phones with good cameras on these days so why not use your own photos and start building up your own library of images? Flickr creative commons is also a good option for images you can use with permission, see **http://www.flickr.com/creativecommons/** . Stock image websites are big business and come in all shapes and sizes. I use Big Stock Photo as they are user-friendly and great value compared to many out there. You can use the link below to get 20% off one of their image packs: **http://www. bigstockphoto.com/promo/PRE51Ns**

This chapter is an expert from my book *PowerPoint Surgery: How to create presentation slides that make your message stick.* Available from Amazon or directly from my website **www. leejackson.biz**

"Lee Jackson is the man who takes PowerPoint presentations from boring to brilliant. If you take his straightforward advice, your audiences will love you, and your messages will hit home. I can't recommend him highly enough. Whether you're pitching for business, delivering internal presentations or speaking to conferences, Lee's advice will make you more successful." Alan Stevens FPSA, Past President Global Speakers Federation and co-author of 'The Exceptional Speaker'.

LEE JACKSON *FPSA*

Lee Jackson is a motivational speaker, PowerPoint surgeon and presentation coach. He's been speaking up front for more than twenty years in many challenging situations. As well as speaking himself, he loves helping other people to speak well too. He is a fellow of the Professional Speaking Association (PSA) and also the president of the PSA Yorkshire region. He supports the New York Knicks, is a former youth worker and was once an award winning DJ.

You can get in touch with him here:

EMAIL: *lee@leejackson.biz*

WEBSITE: *leejackson.biz*

TWITTER: *@leejackson*

CHAPTER ELEVEN

Being the Authentic You as a Speaker

JANE GUNN *FPSA*

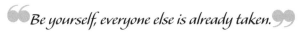

Be yourself, everyone else is already taken.

MIKE ROBBINS

What is it that makes YOU unique as a speaker? Imagine that you're standing in the wings, waiting to go on stage, the conference MC gives you a rousing introduction, the audience claps in anticipation and you walk on stage into the spotlight. Whatever your subject, however powerful your argument, the focus is on YOU!

As speakers, we are told that the audience remembers very little of the content that we deliver. There are of course tips and techniques to help us improve retention rates. What people do remember however, is how you made them FEEL. And how we make our audience feel depends entirely on WHO we are and how much of our true and authentic selves we are prepared to reveal to them.

Authenticity

So who are you as you step up on stage and deliver your speech? Are you your Professional Speaker self with a carefully crafted message designed to motivate and inspire? Are you your Professional Expert self with information and data to persuade and challenge? Or do you dare to be just you?

3 Stages of Development

Let's begin by looking at how we develop as speakers. The process seems to involve three major stages. Although these are described sequentially, they may overlap or occur simultaneously.

First, as new speakers, we study technique. We learn about stagecraft, how to stand and move as we speak and interact with the audience. We learn how to use our voice and how to breathe, we learn how to write our speech and how to remember it and we learn about using props and audio-visuals. And then we look for opportunities to try out those techniques.

The second stage of our development as speakers involves working towards a deeper understanding of how and why our presentations work and how we can adapt, change and customize to suit each audience that we work with. As we become more comfortable with our material and being in front of an audience, we can start to fine-tune, perhaps add humour or a new opening or close.

The third and perhaps the most challenging stage of our development as speakers is a growing awareness of how our own personal and unique qualities influence our performance – for better or worse!

It is at this stage that we begin to focus on and take responsibility for our own personal development as speakers.

Being, Not Doing

It was a Regional PSA meeting and several of the group's Associate Members had signed up to deliver a 10-minute Showcase. One at a time the members came up and delivered their presentations and then it was Mike's turn. During the other presentations, I could see Mike out of the corner of my eye, shuffling the prompt cards that he had prepared as he waited to take his turn. As Mike walked to centre stage to take his turn he held on tight to his cards and as he began to speak. I could see him struggling to remember what was on those cards without needing to take a peak. All of a sudden Mike flung his cards to the ground and said, "I've spent all week preparing for this and writing notes galore. Damn it! Let me just speak from the heart and tell you what I really wanted to say". He then proceeded to tell his story with so much passion, that the audience was captivated.

Was Mike's presentation word perfect? No, it was not! Did he remember everything he had planned to say? Probably not! Was his stagecraft faultless? I don't think it was. But the truth is I don't remember those things. What I do remember is an authentic presentation, delivered from the heart and that's what mattered most.

The point is that speaking is about *BEING* who we truly are rather than simply *DOING* certain prescribed steps. Does that mean that stagecraft and all the other speaking skills that we learn don't really matter? Not at all! BUT in addition to what the speaker does, is the matter of who the speaker is. It is the speaker's being as experienced by the audience that sends the message. It is our unique spirit that emanates from who we are not what we do – in other words, from our being.

What Matters Most to You and Why?

Whatever the subject you have chosen to speak about, whether it's sales, branding, leadership, strategy – the thing that interests the audience most is WHY?

Maybe you are an expert in your field, perhaps you have worked for many years at the coal face building up your knowledge and experience but what is it that motivates you to speak on that subject? Why do you want to address audience after audience on that topic?

When I am working with people as a mediator or coach, the question I ask them to focus on is "What matters most to you?" and "Why?"

The problem for many speakers is that they do not have a clear idea about their WHY. They can set a goal or goals for their speaking business but what they are not clear about is what effect or OUTCOME achieving that goal will have on their lives (and on the lives of their audience).

Maybe you dream of speaking to 10,000 people like Tony Robbins, or perhaps your goal is to develop a series of masterclasses for business leaders. Whatever your dream or goal, what is it that you will achieve as a result? For most people, the OUTCOME is very different from the stated dream or goal.

The simple but provocative question is "If I obtained this goal, what would I get?"

When you are able to answer this, then repeat the question with the new result and so on until you get to the essence of what you really want.

Here is a typical example of this conversation with my 20-year old self.

"What do you want, Jane?"

"I want a sports car" – I could describe it in detail, including the colour and the upholstery. It was a white, soft-top MG.

"Let's say you had that sports car Jane, what would you get by having it?"

"Well, I'd get to drive around in it and people would notice it and say "Wow!""

"Ah, I see. What you really want is more people to notice you. And if you had more people noticing you Jane, what would you get from that?"

"Well, to tell you the truth, if I had more people noticing me..........perhaps Paul would notice me too"

"Ah, what you really want is Paul to notice you. So if you had Paul paying attention to you, what would you get from that?"

"Yes, well ...."

"Well, Jane, let's say you got that. What would you really get from that?"

"Well, if I got that, really had Paul noticing me and even going out with me, I guess what I'd get is....... I'd get to feel OK, like I was really somebody"

"So what you really want is to be somebody. If you were somebody what would you get?"

"I think what I'd get, if I were somebody, is I'd get to feel good about myself. I'd start to really like myself and know that I was OK"

Now we're getting close to the heart of the vision of my 20-year old self.

"So what you really want Jane is to know that you're OK, to like yourself, to love yourself even?"

"So Jane, if you had all this love for yourself, all this respect for yourself, what would you do with it all?"

"I think if I really loved myself, I'd find it easier to give that love to others. Because I'd be happy with myself, I'd able to create more happiness around me"

The outcome of this exercise is always similar. Why not try it yourself? You will move from a specific WANT – a standing ovation, a shiny car, a £ million pound business, into knowing what you really NEED – and it's almost always a quality of being and a sense of being able to GIVE to others.

Discovering Your Authentic Self

Authenticity describes a genuineness, a truthfulness and a congruence in our communications and behaviours with our own values and beliefs and with the situation and people with whom we are interacting.

So how do you discover your authenticity?

What unique qualities or style do you possess that makes you who you are?

Patricia Fripp is, according to Meetings and Conventions magazine, "One of the most electrifying speakers in North America" - she is also a highly sought-after executive speech coach. One of Patricia's many content development suggestions is the *Once Upon a Time Technique* which is like a Fairy Story. As children all stories started with something like this..."Once upon a time there was a princess living in a castle in the heart of the forest...."

Patricia suggests that you make a time line overview for your most vivid memories, major influencers, learning lessons, turning points and vivid reflections of your life; starting from "Where did you grow up, what did your parents do, what advice did they give you?"

Then if you run it by a friend you will discover based on what they ask, what an audience would be curious about.

As you retrace your life's journey thus far, what personal qualities most define you? How would others describe you? Make a list of these qualities. It may include some of the following:

- *Humility*
- *Fun/humour*
- *Curiosity*
- *Wisdom*
- *Patience*
- *Service*

Another exercise you can do is to think about times and situations when you feel you are at your most and when you are at your least authentic?

Whenever I have done this exercise with people, they tend to describe a time when they felt at their most authentic, in other words when they were most able to be themselves and who they truly are, when they did not feel under pressure to meet other people's expectations and values, instead of being true to their own. On the other hand, they felt at their most authentic when they felt at peace with themselves and the world around them.

The Speaker's "Presence"

Can you think of a speaker who seems to be totally present, in the moment when they speak?

When you experience this kind of speaker, it feels as though they are speaking just to you. You get a deep sense that they care about you personally, that they share your hopes and understand your concerns.

Being fully present as a speaker means being congruent with your own values, beliefs and higher purpose. It means connecting with the humanity of others and being respectful of their own values and beliefs. Presence means behaving in a manner that includes every member of your audience regardless of their background, status or appearance.

The audience knows on an intuitive level whether you are truly there with them – communicating openly, honestly and genuinely.

The challenge for all of us is that presence and connection is about vulnerability. It means allowing ourselves to be seen – really seen for who we are. It means having the courage to be imperfect. To truly connect, we must be prepared to reveal our true selves – our hopes and fears, our differences and divisions, our dreams and our desires.

If you don't let your own barrier down then people will not hear you!

Your Journey to Mastery

Success is a journey – not a destination!

From the moment we are born, we learn through experience and by responding to challenges and struggles that we have fought with ourselves. Qualities and values such as empathy, trust, flexibility, humour and so on can be learnt and may often be modelled by others but they cannot be taught as such. As Oscar Wilde once said "Nothing worth knowing can be taught".

In order to deepen our understanding of the psychological, intellectual and spiritual qualities that make us who we are and to continue our journey of self-development, we may need to reach beyond the traditional boundaries of speaking and broaden our knowledge by learning from other traditions. Psychotherapy, quantum physics, systems analysis, chaos theory, religious discipline, NLP, yoga and meditation may each have something to add. There are many paths to greater self-awareness. What is important however is that the learning is both self-managed and self-directed with opportunities for reflection particularly as it relates to the self as a speaker.

Who we are and the personal qualities that we bring into the room or onto the speaking platform are ultimately what enable our ability to help others make sense of their own views and perceptions of the world. This is our work and our journey as speakers. Part of this work and of our continual growth must be to constantly be open to learning from others, no matter how experienced we may be.

Self-awareness, presence, authenticity, congruence, integration are some of the qualities the development of which may help us on the journey to being rather than doing and thus to personal mastery.

The place to begin is not with a set of ideal personal qualities to which we vainly aspire, but with the arduous practical struggle to live every day consistent with our values, ethics and integrity.

In a Nutshell

Authenticity is about being who we are and sharing our unique experiences, challenges and lessons from a place of vulnerability and humility that can enable us to truly connect with the pain and needs as well as the hopes and dreams of our audience.

What, if anything, is holding you back from being the most authentic, vital you as a speaker?

> 66 *Be the person you intended to be before you intended to be the person you are not. It is time to seek authenticity in ourselves and remove all masks.* 99
>
> **DANIELLE MAYLYN**

JANE GUNN *FPSA*

Jane Gunn, the Corporate Peacemaker is a highly sought after mediator and professional speaker. She specialises in collaboration, dynamic dialogue and transforming business relationships and has helped numerous companies to move from deadlock situations to opening new streams of revenue and a vibrant corporate culture. Saving her clients thousands of £'s, tiresome lawsuits, devastating disputes and ruined relationships on the way.

Jane travels and speaks all over the world. She has been invited to speak at the White House, the United Nations and the European Commission. She is currently President Elect of the Professional Speaking Association and is one of just 7 women Fellows. She is also a member of the Global Speakers Federation.

As one of the leading Mediators in the UK, she has over 16 years' experience, and has mediated a wide variety of disputes including, business, partnership, employment, property and construction, personal injury and clinical negligence, trusts and family disputes.

Accredited by CEDR in 1996 she is a Mediator Fellow of the Chartered Institute of Arbitrators and an International Mediation Institute (IMI) Certified International Mediator

Jane is also the author of the recently published book on conflict management *How to Beat Bedlam in the Boardroom and Boredom in the Bedroom.*

You can contact Jane by:

EMAIL: ***jane.gunn@corpeace.com***

PHONE: ***+44 (0)1491 874 070***

WEBSITE: ***www.corpeace.com***

TWITTER: ***@janegunn***

LinkedIn and Facebook

CHAPTER TWELVE

How to Maximise your Revenue from Every Speaking Opportunity

SIMON ZUTSHI *MPSA*

As a professional speaker you can be very well financially rewarded for sharing your knowledge and experience with your audience.

Traditionally the main source of income for most professional speakers has been from delivering keynote presentations to corporate organisations. However, more and more speakers are now increasing their overall speaking revenue through alternative income streams, which will be the main focus of this chapter.

Adding more value to your audience

When you are paid thousands of pounds to deliver a keynote presentation, the organisation is not just paying you for the 45 minutes of your time but rather for your years of experience and more importantly the value, wisdom and inspiration you can transfer to the audience.

No matter how good a speaker you are, there is only going to be certain amount you can achieve in such a short space of time. Your audience may be informed, educated and inspired to do things differently as a direct result of your presentation, but let's be realistic here, how long will the effect of your message last after you have delivered it?

There is a way for you to deliver even more value to your clients with sustainability by also providing further support in the form of products, consulting, coaching and workshops. I don't know of many speakers who make a living just from delivering their 45 minute keynote presentations alone. All truly successful speakers I know have other products and services to complement their keynotes.

Increasing your revenue whenever you speak

As speakers we want to have a lasting positive impact on our audiences. The best way to achieve this is though products and services.

In chapter 4, Mindy mentioned how she and her clients bundle books into a package with a keynote to increase the revenue and value to the client. I would recommend all speakers aim to write at least one really good book on your specialist topic. It is not only great supporting material but it will also boost your credibility as a speaker.

I was attending the National Speakers Association annual convention in Philadelphia this summer, and in one of the workshops, a very successful speaker shared how using her product, an on-line assessment tool, to differentiate herself from other speakers and massively increases the amount she makes when she speaks. She sells this online assessment to her client and if they buy enough of them then she includes her keynote as a bonus. This is just a different way of packaging your services.

Ideally, the best way to increase your revenue is to get the organiser to pay for additional products/services in advance. However, depending on the event you may be allowed to promote your products and services for sale at the back of the room. This can work really well when members of the audience are interested in their own ongoing personal development. Good examples of this are sales people or people involved in the multi-level marketing businesses.

If you are going to sell products at the back of the room you need to make sure it is appropriate and you get permission from the client in advance. My personal experience is that the more value you provide in your presentation, the more the delegates want to learn more from you.

If you are speaking at a paid event where it is not appropriate to sell your products and services at the back of the room, an alternative idea is to offer a complimentary follow up webinar in the week after your speaking engagement.

You will know that the people who bother to listen in to your free webinar will probably be the ones who gained the most from your keynote. You could make an offer to the participants of this webinar, giving them the opportunity to buy additional webinars, products and or services. I would still recommend that you seek permission from the client to do this promotion within the webinar as you don't want to upset them in any way.

There are some events (generally ones open to the public rather than corporate ones), where the event promoter will expect you to sell your products and give them a commission from the sales. This is how they make their money from these events, which are often free or low cost to attend.

You need to make sure that your presentation does not become a sales pitch. Most people hate being sold to. However,

I have found that if you can give real value to your audience and demonstrate your expertise many people will want to get more help from you and so be interested in what you have to offer.

This year I was asked to speak at a very large event for property investors in London. This is my niche market and I am fairly well known in the UK so the organisers wanted me to speak as a draw to bring in delegates, but also they wanted me to promote their event to my clients. I was paid a good fee to speak and told that I was not allowed to promote any products apart from my book. So I gave massive value with the result that, after my presentation I was contacted by several people who had been in the audience, who had spoken to some of my clients who were also in the audience and wanted to do some further training with me. The result was that I was earned an additional £8k to £10k on top of my speaking fee.

A fellow speaker, Jo Simpson, who is a leading authority on Values, spoke at one of my events a few months ago. She was asked not to promote anything and as usual gave a fantastic presentation. After she had finished her talk, she was invited back onto the stage by the MC who asked her how people could learn more from her! She mentioned her amazing one-day Values Discovery workshop that she runs and made a great offer to my delegates. The result was that she made an additional £5000 in workshop sales without really doing a heavy sales pitch.

Making money when speaking for free!

I was once advised that one of the best ways to improve your speaking is to speak as much as you possibly can. The more you speak, the more experience you gain, the more your confidence grows, the more you learn what works and what does not work for your audience.

Of course when you first start to speak, it may be hard to find people who are prepared to pay you. You may need to do a number of free presentations, or rather "showcases" as we refer to them in the Professional Speaking Association until you reach the point where you are good enough for someone to pay you to speak to their organisation.

If you doing a showcase, then I believe it is perfectly reasonable for you to ask for the opportunity to make an appropriate offer to the audience, if they are interested in learning more from you.

Here are some tips for selling in showcases:

1. *Pack as much value into your talk as possible*

2. *Subtly mention your services throughout your talk (e.g. a case study of how you have helped someone)*

3. *Pack as much value into your talk as possible*

4. *Save enough time at the end for your offer*

5. *Pack as much value into your talk as possible*

6. *Make an "elegant, irresistible, no-brainer" offer*

Oh...... and did I mention, most important to make sure you provide massive value in your talk so that people think "Wow, if I have learnt this much in this talk, I wonder how much I could learn if I spent more time with them?

An alternative revenue model for speakers

The majority of my speaking opportunities are "showcases", in other words speaking opportunities for which I am not paid to speak, and yet I am probably one of the highest earning speakers in the UK.

How is this possible? Whenever I speak, I make money but not necessarily in the conventional way of being paid for delivering a keynote presentation.

I have a slightly different model from most of the other speakers featured in this book. Instead of speaking to companies and organisations I spend most of my time speaking directly to consumers. Specifically, individuals who want to learn about my area of expertise which is successful real estate investing. I have been investing in property since 1995 and became financially independent at the age of 32 thanks to the passive income from my property portfolio.

Since 2003 I have been helping other people to achieve what I did, but in far less time than it took me. I give away a huge amount of valuable information for free through my webinars, my blog, articles in property magazines and of course speaking at related events.

I have developed a number of products and services to help people become more successful investors ranging from: a low entry price for my book, and Audio CDs, to a midrange investment for my home study programmes, one-day and three-day seminars up to a higher investment to join my 12-month property mastermind programme.

It should go without saying - but I think I need to mention just in case, that you must only offer quality products to your clients or you might as well not bother.

The key to developing any good product is to give far more value than the investment needed to acquire the product. If you are giving more value than you receive for your product then customers will want to keep buying your products.

How to get paid when you are not there!

As speakers we can get paid a very high hourly rate. However most speakers are still trading their time for money. Your earnings are capped to the amount of time you have available. If you are not speaking, you are not earning.

This is why creating your own products is one of the best things you can do. It does take some time and effort but all you have to do is work once to create a product for which you could get paid forever.

It is very easy to get overwhelmed by the thought of having to create products such as audio CDs, DVDs, seminars and workshops, in addition to putting together a fantastic keynote presentation.

The good news is that creating your own products can actually be as simple as filming one of your presentations. This recording can then be made into a DVD. The audio could be used to create a CD or podcast, and the audio can be transcribed by someone to create an e-book or workbook.

A good habit to get into is to record all of your talks on a simple voice recorder. There are two benefits of this. 1) You might be able to create it into an audio product. 2) Listening to a recording of your own talk is a great way to learn how you can improve your content and presentation.

Another easy way of creating a product is to record a webinar. This is very straightforward to do. As long as you can put together a content rich PowerPoint presentation (or Keynote for Mac) then you have all you need to run a webinar. I use **http://www.gotowebinar.com** who even offer a 30-day free trial of the service.

A final word of advice here. When creating your products, don't try to get it perfect. A finished (slightly non perfect) product is better than one that you have not released yet (because it is not quite right). Even if you get close to your perfect product, a year later you probably will be an even better speaker and want to do it again anyway. Just do it and get it out there.

In summary:

By creating your own products and services and offering them to your clients, to complement your talks, you can provide extra value and longer lasting impact on your audiences whilst earning extra revenue. A win/win for everyone!

SIMON ZUTSHI MPSA

Simon Zutshi, experienced investor, successful entrepreneur, and best-selling author, is a dynamic, passionate and inspirational speaker widely recognised as one of the top wealth creation specialists in the UK.

He became financially independent by the age of 32 having started to invest in 1995. Passionate about sharing his experience, Simon founded the property investor's network (www.joinpin.co.uk) in 2003 which has grown to become the largest property networking organisation in the UK, with monthly meetings in 40 cities, designed specifically to provide a supportive, educational and inspirational environment for people like you to network with and learn from other successful investors.

Since 2003 Simon has taught thousands of entrepreneurs and business owners how to successfully invest in a tax efficient way to create additional streams of passive income, give them more time to do the things they want to do and build their long-term wealth, whilst helping other people at the same time.

Simon's first book *Property Magic* which is now in its fourth edition became an instant hit when first released in 2008 and remains an Amazon No. 1 bestselling property book.

You can find out more about Simon and his speaking here:

WEBSITE: **www.SimonZutshi.com**

WEBSITE: **www.Property-Mastermind.com**

TWITTER: **@simonzutshi**

LINKEDIN: **www.linkedin.com/in/simonzutshi**

CHAPTER THIRTEEN

Making Conscious Choices in Your Speaking Business...

JO SIMPSON *MPSA*

How do you know when to say 'Yes' or 'No' to the exciting yet sometimes overwhelming number of choices available to you as a professional speaker?

When we start out, it is so very tempting to say yes to everything that comes our way, but is that always the right thing for us to do? Sometimes this can be helpful in deciding what works and what doesn't, but it's important to remember that every decision we make has an impact on who we are as a speaker, what we offer, our brand and our reputation. So it's a good idea to take some time out in advance (or for existing speakers, the next best time to do this is now!) to define or re-define who you want to be as a speaker, what topic(s) you speak on and to set some boundaries so that the power of saying Yes or indeed No, becomes second nature.

Have you ever said 'Yes' and then kicked yourself afterwards, because with hindsight you wished you had said 'No'; but maybe in the moment, you wanted to help someone out, were eager to please or thought it was a great income opportunity? Or have you said 'No' to something, possibly out of fear or thinking you weren't experienced enough and realised later on that in fact it was a great opportunity and with a little more self-belief, 'Yes' would have been a better answer for you.

My aim for this chapter is to get you thinking more consciously about the choices you make in your speaking business and asking yourself if they are aligned to who you are and the area you specialise in. We are all faced with many choices every day; specifically I am going to focus on four key areas that impact speakers on a regular basis. These are: Your Speaking Topic; When and Where to Speak; How you spend your time (in/out and on your business) and whom to form Collaborations/Joint Ventures with. I will also be including a framework with which to help you define which are the right choices for you and set your boundaries accordingly.

Your Speaking Topic

Before defining your speaking topic, the first question you need to answer is WHY?

Why do you want to speak? This is essential as a basis to make conscious choices from. Is it because you are passionate about a certain topic based on your own experiences? Or because you think Speaking is a great way to get recognition or make money? Is it because you have a message to share with the world and want to make a positive difference to other's lives? It may be one or more of the above or something else that is not mentioned here. It is really important to define this, as it is linked to your purpose and your personal drivers – When our choices are aligned to these, not only are they the right ones, you will feel rewarded and fulfilled in your business.

To Niche or Not to Niche?

That is the question I have heard probably the most often in my speaking career. Should you pick a niche area and stick to it or diversify and see what sticks? If you do choose to niche, then how far do you take this... What do you want to be known for?

For example, are you a speaker who is an expert in sales? And you have chosen sales as your niche. This may be too wide an area and it's worth considering if there is a specific area of sales you specialise in, i.e. closing sales or the business development aspect of sales, or do you go further and micro-niche to 'closing sales for technology companies?' This is your choice to make and if you are currently not sure, observe what flows to you and notice who you naturally attract as clients, as there will be several clues here, as illustrated in my own example below.

My own niche is in the area of values-based leadership, not just leadership! There are thousands of leadership speakers, so it's important that I define myself in my specialist area. I didn't consciously start my speaking business with a niche area in mind; it evolved over the years and the benefit of hindsight is a wonderful thing. I realised that in my speaking and coaching business, there was a strong resonance to the piece I covered on values, so on deeper reflection across all the clients I have worked with and my own journey, whereby discovering values had a huge impact on the choices I made in my business and life in general. It was already there staring me in the face – What is it that is so obvious to you, that's staring you in the face? What do you get feedback and testimonials on the most from your clients? This could very well be your niche area.

The choice to micro-niche?

Most of my own clients used to be mainly in the banking and financial sectors, as that is my background. At one point I was pondering on the idea on whether to micro-niche in this area and then various different companies started to approach me who weren't in this sector, and I made a conscious choice that if organisations were wanting to take a deeper look at their leaders values and those of the organisation, I was not going to say "No, sorry I only work with banks". I checked in with my personal motivators (my core values) and my purpose of 'Helping leaders to live and lead in line with who they truly are' and narrowing to banks and finance companies only would have been a dis-service to other forward-thinking organisations that wanted to bring about transformation in their leadership teams.

Having defined your topic and your niche area, this will form a great foundation for making conscious choices in the next section.

When & Where to speak

When?

Do you accept every opportunity that comes your way? And then get the learning's as to whether you want to repeat similar opportunities again or do you make a conscious choice in advance to only accept speaking gigs that are in line with your topic, your niche area and your core values. Sometimes we get our best learning's by just going out there and going for it, but if you want to be a little more conscious about saying Yes or No, consider the following:

What if you were offered a speaking gig on a topic that isn't your specialist area, not what you are known for, but it's good money – do you take the risk and do it as a one-off? It could affect your brand and your reputation if you do and send out confusing messages, not to mention that you may not do your best job if it's not your specialist area that you live and breathe by.

I have been asked in the past to deliver a keynote on the subject of mindset and while this is part of the coaching work I do, it isn't the area I specialise in, so I make a conscious choice to say No and recommend a fellow PSA speaker, who does specialise in this area. This creates a win-win-win, the meeting planner sees you as a true professional for sticking to your area of expertise, another speaker gets a gig (I only recommend if I have seen someone speak and value what they do and how they do it) and you gain credibility and respect. You are likely to be remembered for gigs that are more suitable for you in the future by the meeting planner or booker, and as an extra bonus, the speaker you recommended may just reciprocate in the future.

'No Fee' Speaking? Or A Showcase?

An interesting exercise in saying Yes or No is when you are asked to speak for 'No Fee' – notice I didn't say speak for free. At the PSA, we call these occasions a showcase – a chance to show people what you do. Again, some thought in advance as to how you make the choice could include – will there be decision makers in the room who may book you for other events? Is it the first time you have delivered this particular keynote? In which case it may be a good opportunity to deliver live for the first time (very important to ensure you have still put the necessary preparation in though!). Or is it a charity that it dear to your heart and it's important to you that you speak for them. You may also want to consider how many showcases you do a year and set some boundaries / guidelines accordingly. Again, know why you are doing it.

Where do you want to speak?

This is an area that I recommend you give strong consideration to, in advance. Do you want to speak locally, nationally, globally or all of the above? What is important to you about where you speak? I have seen many speakers be drawn to speaking internationally, and again as long as you know your 'reason why / your purpose', this can be extremely exciting and rewarding, meeting new people, experiencing different cultures and getting your message out to other parts of the globe. On the flip side, it can mean days at a time away from your family, travelling alone and potential opportunity costs with travel days being added on to the trip (unless of course, you can negotiate for your booker to pay you for these too)

Last year, I made a conscious choice to speak in Iran, as it was completely in line with all my personal drivers (core values) and purpose. I love speaking internationally, but only if it is a fit for me. I have also chosen consciously that I will only spend a certain amount of my time abroad, as I have other areas of my life in the UK that are also very important to me. If you are interested in speaking globally, I highly recommend you become a member of the Global Speakers Federation (**http://www.globalspeakers.net**) and attend speaking conferences in other countries. (I am currently writing this chapter in New York, after attending the National Speakers Association Convention in Philadelphia – another conscious choice I have made to invest in developing myself to be the best speaker I can possibly be).

A fellow speaker friend of mine, loves travelling as it is a lifestyle fit for him, he loves spending time seeing other countries and is consciously building his business through partnering with companies in the countries that have a personal appeal for him. He is very clear on his 'reason why' and indeed his personal drivers and what's more, because he has so much clarity on these areas, it is working extremely well.

'Making Conscious Choices' Framework – DISCOVER, DEFINE, IGNITE ™

This is probably a good point to introduce the 1st step of my framework, which will help you with discovering your own personal drivers. Once discovered, they can be used as a foundation for all the choices you make.

Step 1: DISCOVER

Some questions that will help you start this process are:

● *What is 'important' to you about your speaking business?*

Example answers could include:

That I deliver great keynotes; I earn 'x' amount per year; I get booked regularly, I am known globally, I receive great testimonials and recommendations from my clients

Then break it down further and ask yourself:

- *What do these give / bring me personally?*

The ability to make a positive difference, inspire others, provide (for my family), recognition, achievement, adventure, fun, security, freedom, lifestyle, energy...(*These are likely to be your personal motivators or core values*)

Take some time to create your own answers – we are uncovering here, the essence of what personally drives YOU? (This is essential to know as a basis from which to make conscious choices) We are all unique, so what's right for one person is not necessarily the right choice for you!

Another great question to ask is:

- *What do you 'ENJOY' the most about your speaking business?*

Example answers could be:

Meeting new people, connecting with my audience, getting financially rewarded for something I love, collaborating with fellow speakers and having shared interests.

Again, take some time to create your own.

And the last question, which is often the easiest to answer:

- *What 'FRUSTRATES' you the most about your speaking business?*

Now, before you answer this one, note that once you have the answer, we are going to flip it over to the positive, as this will be one of your personal drivers.

Example answers could be:

People letting you down, disorganised, being told what to do by others.

You could then flip these over to:

- *Reliability*
- *Organisation*
- *Freedom of Choice*

These are likely to be important personal drivers for you.

Once you have worked out what frustrates you and flipped over the answers, you should now have the essence of the areas that are driving your choices, which maybe you weren't conscious of before. The power of knowing what our personal drivers (core values) are, is what will help us to make better decisions from a more informed and conscious perspective.

If the choice you have to make is a fit with these areas, it's a 'Yes' and if not it's a 'No'

Sounds simple and it can be, though there can be times when the choice will meet one of your personal drivers and possibly not another. BUT at least you are able to make an informed choice and know consciously why you are making the choice, that if for example you do 'x', you will be fulfilling your 'adventure' and 'freedom' drivers, but maybe not your security one. It is through making informed and conscious choices that we feel less angst and inner conflict, because we are in control of what we are doing and why we are doing it.

Intuition...

This also has a big part to play in making conscious choices, as our core values are our intuition made conscious. Do you ever have a feeling that something is not right and you should say no – this is your intuition guiding you (usually we can highlight this better when reflecting on previous choices and we say – "something was telling me I should have done that and I didn't listen to it") conversely, you may also get a very excited feeling when you know something is right and the more you learn to trust this, the more powerful your choices become. This is where checking-in with your core values really supports your intuition. Your intuition is not tangible, it's a feeling, if you have taken time to discover and define your values, you can consciously check in with them to see if indeed it is the right decision for you.

How You Spend Your Time

By now, you should have a very clear idea of what's important to you, what you enjoy (this is the stuff that truly energises us) and what frustrates the 'bleep bleep' out of you too (this is a good indication of what you may want to outsource ;-)

Use this as a basis for how to spend your time. I am guessing that most of you would love to spend most of your time speaking and that may be possible for some, but generally most Speakers offer a cross-section of services – keynotes, master classes, workshops, 1-1 coaching.

Do you love to spend your time writing as well as speaking? As Mindy said, speakers often hear "You should have a book." Please check-in with yourself here; if it's important to you and you have a desire to write a book – do it, but don't do it because you feel 'you should' as it won't be aligned to your personal drivers and ultimately will not be fulfilling. In fact, don't do anything, because you feel you 'should' or 'ought' to do it, I guarantee this will not get you the desired results.

You will also need to factor in creative time for your writing, preparing keynotes, master classes, blogs, social media, prospecting new business, proposals, admin, financials – you are a business owner as well as speaker!

Choose the work that brings you alive and energises you in all you do and outsource the rest. This may be a parallel process for a while, as I appreciate funds are needed to outsource, but don't let this put you off – the more you can outsource, the more time you have to focus on doing what you love, your unique abilities and what you are great at. When you do this, you are aligned and you increase the possibilities of more of what you love flowing to you.

Whom to Collaborate / Joint Venture with...

You may want to collaborate with other speakers at times or joint venture with someone such as a marketing director or business development director, who can you help grow your business.

This is a good stage to introduce the second step of the framework to make conscious choices about whom you choose to work with. Once you have discovered your own personal drivers, it is important that any potential collaborators / business partners do the same, but that's not enough! Have you ever been in a partnership or joint venture that has gone wrong? I certainly have and know many others that have experienced this, and while initially it's all exciting and you appear to want the same things, further down the line, things have changed and you are not sure what has happened.

So, yes it's important to have shared / complementary core values (personal motivators), but you need to take them one step further and define what they mean to you individually and together.

Step 2 – DEFINE

Example – let's say you have a core value of 'Freedom' and you both agree that Freedom is important to you in your business.

Then ask the all-important question:

● *'What does 'Freedom' mean to you?*

To Person A – It may mean Freedom of Choice

To Person B – It could mean Freedom to travel and have a relaxed lifestyle.

These are two very different meanings and if not defined, this could not only cause a conflict with each other, but also has an impact to what you say 'Yes' or 'No' to.

It's worth taking some time to expand on step one and ask yourself – 'What does X mean to me? (Replace X with all of your discovered personal motivators, 1 by 1) This enables you to clearly DEFINE their meanings and set clear boundaries for yourself and others.

I also recommend discovering and defining a set of joint core values for any business partnerships and joint ventures that all business decisions then can be based on.

Mastermind Groups and Joining the PSA

This chapter would not be complete without me recommending you consciously choose to join or create a speaker mastermind group and become a member of your local Professional Speaking Association. As speakers, it can be a lonely business and the power of meeting on a regular basis with other speakers to share ideas, debate, give and receive advice and of course mastermind with like-minded people who have your best interests at heart, is extremely powerful. I have personally gained immense value, professionally and personally from being part of my mastermind group (all of whom I met through the PSA) and indeed on a wider basis, the Professional Speaking Association.

To join or create a mastermind group, use the collaboration guidelines above to choose like-minded, like hearted people, who have a common purpose.

STEP 3 - IGNITE

The final step in my 'Framework to make Conscious Choices' is to Ignite them and by this I mean, make them alive and active in all that you do:

- *Make conscious choices based on your core values*

- *Set your goals and vision in alignment with them (you are much more likely to achieve them and enjoy the process if you do)*

- *Make courageous decisions, which may seem scary at the time – Trust that if they are in line with your values, they will work out.*

- *Improve your Relationships through understanding yourself and others better – Business and Personal*

- *Select the best collaborations and Joint Ventures for you*

- *Hire your outsource team in alignment with what's important to you and ensure they have shared, complimentary values.*

I use this framework myself and with my clients. This helps them make more courageous and conscious choices in their leadership and the results of what happens when DISCOVER, DEFINE and IGNITE your personal motivators (core values) in this way are phenomenal. Not only will you feel more confident and powerful about the choices you make, you will build a speaking business that is built on solid sustainable foundations, and you will enjoy the process which is extremely rewarding and personally fulfilling too.

Have fun making Conscious Choices and do let me know the results you get!

JO SIMPSON *MPSA*

Jo Simpson is a leading authority in aligning Leaders with their Values. Throughout her 25-year career, she has led countless corporate teams to greater success through the application of her innovative approach to leadership and executive management practices.

Jo's background is in banking and whilst she has an impressive track record in managing training teams, facilitating, designing, and delivering education programs, it was her journey to Dubai in 2005 that inspired her to create her leadership coaching and speaking business. Jo helped to transform the business and management culture of numerous international and locally based organisations through her pioneering approach. Jo fast became a regular and very popular speaker at leadership and organisational conferences. Jo has developed the skills of over five thousand Leaders to make more courageous and conscious choices in their leadership, creating sustainable culture changes and adopting coaching styles in the workplace.

Companies that have entrusted Jo with their most prized assets – their people – include Halifax plc, Credit Suisse, LloydsTSB, Barclays Bank, KPMG, ABN-AMRO, Microsoft, Nokia, L'Oreal, Smith and Nephew, GlaxoSmithKline, Hewlett Packard, Rolls-Royce plc & Cisco, to name a few.

Jo is now based in the UK. She is a founder member of the PSA Middle East, a member of the PSA UKI and a representative for the Global Speakers Federation.

To find about more about Jo,

EMAIL: *info@josimpson.com*

PHONE: *+44 121 369 1544*

WEBSITES: *www.josimpson.com and www.valuesdiscovery.com*

LINKED IN: *www.linkedin.com/in/josimpson*

TWITTER: *@josimpsonspeaks*

FACEBOOK: *www.facebook.com/josimpsonuk*